OWL MEETS ALIEN

Amongst others
on my soul's journey

By

Margarite Westo

© 2003 by Margarite Westo. All rights reserved.

No part of this book may be reproduced, stored in a retrieval system, or transmitted by any means, electronic, mechanical, photocopying, recording, or otherwise, without written permission from the author.

ISBN: 1-4107-2551-0 (e-book)
ISBN: 1-4107-2550-2 (Paperback)
ISBN: 1-4107-4288-1 (Dust Jacket)

Library of Congress Control Number: 2003091293

This book is printed on acid free paper.

Printed in the United States of America
Bloomington, IN

1stBooks - rev. 04/11/03

SPECIAL NOTE

If you have a medical issue or illness, consult a qualified doctor.

The material in this book is not intended as medical advice, nor does it take the place of a physician but works alongside.

The names of clients have been changed and certain details omitted to protect their privacy.

I wish to express my gratitude to those who have allowed me to serve them in a healing and teaching way over the years, and those friends that have encouraged and helped me in the production of this book.

CONTENTS

Preface vii
Introduction xi
My Own Awakening 1
The Healing Experience 9
Why Are There Two? 18
The Journey of the Soul 19
Evolving the Senses 23
Guidance 27
Soul Path Clearing 31
My Own Battle with Illness 38
My Healing 45
What Do I Mean By Self? 49
Energy 51
Cleansing Our Energy 54
Clearing Land and Buildings 56
Making Those Energetic Connections 61
The Mental Body 66
Creative Thought 69
The Emotional Body 71
Getting Help 74
Prayer As A Healer 78
Letting Go 79

Forgiveness Formula 81
Cutting the Links 84
The Spiritual Body 89
The Healing Exercise 91
Introduction to the Sessions 97
Learn to Fly 100
Delia's Magic Man 103
Lingering Death 107
Off the Path! 111
Pride Takes a Fall 113
Dovey, Family Ties 115
The Acceptance of Power 118
The Big Snake 120
The Blindman 125
The Three 129
Sex, What a Mess! 133
Don't Carry that Restriction with You 137
The Balloon Method 140
If I Should Leave Before You Say Goodbye 143

PREFACE

It was 1970 when I was invited to spend a weekend in Walberswick, Suffolk at the studio and home of an artist friend. I had wanted to visit the area as it is known as Turner country, and I loved Turner's paintings. My friend was having two Indian Tantric artists as her guests and she had invited a few artist friends she thought would be interested to join them and learn about this sacred Hindu art. As we gathered in the main part of the studio to listen to one of them speak, I felt quite self-conscious being among some quite successful and intellectual artists. Although I painted I did not consider myself an artist, just as I couldn't come to terms with being called a musician in spite of the fact that I played and wrote music. For some reason I was really self-conscious about any creative work, so true to form I found a seat at the back.

One of the Indian gentlemen had not been speaking for very long when he turned to me and pointing his long bony finger in my direction he asked if he could see my hands. To my embarrassment I had to stand up for him to get a good view of me. I placed my hands out in front of me palms up. 'Yes, yes,' he said excitedly, 'You are a remarkable woman. One day you will write a book of philosophy, which will be read by many, and this book will bring them the help they need.'

I sat down without commenting, as I did not understand what on earth he was talking about. What he said obviously impressed me, for over the years I have found his words popping into my head at the most unusual times. I have never been allowed to forget that exchange of energy between us. It was years later and after more references by psychics to a book I was to write, that I could see that there might be a possibility of this happening. I previously thought that to write a book of philosophy one must be like Plato, a scholar and an intellectual. I did not see myself as either of these things, and although I had a great interest in ancient history, art, and music, there was no way I considered I could write anything of a serious nature. I did not imagine I could possibly achieve what I saw to be such a great task, considering I was a lousy speller, and I couldn't even type.

It is over now, but the fear that the thought of performing this task instilled in me in the beginning was the very thing that was stopping me from writing it at all. At that time I had no idea that we could tap into knowledge from anywhere other than our minds, or that word processing and spell checkers would be invented! Nor did I realize that I would have such a remarkable Spiritual awakening.

I thank all of the wonderful teachers I have encountered throughout my life, including patients and students. It is the exchanges with these people that allowed the knowledge I had buried deep in my consciousness to surface. I would also like to acknowledge all the unseen help of my guides, angels and masters. Where would I be without them?

Margarite

INTRODUCTION

Through healing sessions I have learned the soul is energy, formless and intangible. The soul path is a continuous series of experiences. The aim is to eventually merge with the Universal energies, the Divine Mother/Father Spirit, the energy our society calls GOD. One does not lose his/her identities during the process; for instance, I find that while in this lifetime, I can tap into my other life personalities with ease.

At times the soul brings in other energies, or souls, to channel knowledge to and through me to aid in whatever healing is required. I have experienced going into semi trance during a healing session to enable a Spiritual teacher from the higher realms to speak directly to the client. I am aware of everything that is said during this time as I do not lose control of my mind or body. Instead I allow them to be shared by the visiting spirit. I seldom go into full trance as I wish to take full responsibility for what passes through my lips.

Not all communications are from a teaching spirit sometimes we learn from loved ones that have passed over. In these cases the visits are beneficial for both the giver and the receiver. For instance, I recently attended a talented psychic where both my father and an aunt came through to tell me about how they felt regarding my life. My father begged forgiveness for the way he had treated me stating that at the time he did not understand the spiritual side of life and that he loved me in his own way. My aunt Alice said that she felt so sad that I had been so oppressed as I had been born with a spiritual mission and that she could now see how the oppressing of my spiritual development had caused me so much pain. It seems that this oppression of natural God given gifts caused me to have a life of illness, accidents and several experiences of rape.

Whenever life energies are blocked it works like the dam on a river. It turns the flow in a different direction! In this same session I was instructed by a teaching guide to spread this Truth. It is imperative that all children be allowed to develop their natural abilities in their own time. Instead quite often children suffer as parents pass on their own fears and beliefs.

We all have so much to learn, hidden from us until we are able accept it. Even then it takes time and experience before we receive the understanding. For instance, I have been seen to take on many different bodies when performing transfer healing. Which body usually depends on the client and what they need. There are two that are the most significant ones, an owl and an alien. Although I know these bodies well, I am not always aware of them during the healing and I am quite often surprised who sees me in these forms. I have not yet received the understanding of why this happens, but I am aware that I have released all doubt, and will use any method available to help a soul along its path in whatever form is necessary. Ramala says, "The purpose of any book, of any vision, is simply to stimulate your own knowingness, to bring forth your own aspect of trust." May this book do just that.

MY OWN AWAKENING

I will attempt to explain my understanding and interpretation of the path of the soul. But first I need to tell you how I came to realize that there was a soul path at all.

I was born 'open'. By this I mean I was psychically aware from birth. I was not that happy with being psychic for as a child attending boarding schools, I was often punished for lying when I related my experiences of seeing and speaking with Spirit. It was all so natural to me, I didn't realize I was the only one that experienced their presence, that others did not see them.

When I was only four years old I was sent to St. Paul's convent in Kingston, Surrey, England as a boarder. There were no Catholics anywhere in the family, but it was said that I would get a good education. I missed home so much that I would cry myself to sleep every night. Sister St. James, who slept in our dormitory, would hear me and chastise me for making a noise.

One night I had a visit from an old man. He sat on the end of my bed and spoke comforting words to me. I immediately felt better. To me this did not seem strange. He looked like any old man would with his white hair, suit and tie. At four I had no idea that no men, other than priests were allowed in a convent. The old man visited whenever things got too much for me, and after I had been punished several times for lying, I learned to keep quiet about what I know to be a spirit friends visits.

My mother and two of her sisters had the ability to communicate with spirit, so I was born into a family where being psychic was considered normal. What I experienced being a boarder from four to twelve years old caused me to grow up feeling as though I was abnormal. My first confusion I think. All I really wanted was to fit in and be accepted so I learned to hide any psychic experiences whenever possible, and through my unconscious desire to avoid any further encounters, I began to shut down. By the time I was twenty my closing was complete, and it resulted in my not even wanting to hear about anything psychic.

Years later, in 1970, I went to stay with my uncle Frank whose second wife had recently died. While visiting the hospital he himself had suffered a heart attack at her bedside. The combination of the attack, the injection into his heart to revive him, and the loss of his wife, seemed to have changed him from the vibrant, handsome uncle I used to know, to a man who cared little for cleanliness or life. He lived in a big damp Victorian house built at the top of the cliff in the coastal village of Portreath, Cornwall in the West of England. In Victorian times some eccentric wealthy people would build unusual houses known as follies. Uncle's house was a folly built to resemble a castle. Whoever built it incorporated ramparts, a cannon, and of course a flagpole on the seven-acre plot. Four years of dirt had built up during his wife's cancer and her mother's before her.

I set about getting the big house clean and back in order. It was hard work and it took me a whole month. As I went from room to room cleaning through the house I collected together nine knitted woolen blankets. I found them I felt compelled to add them to my bed. It seemed a strange thing to do and they were very heavy to sleep under, but as I said I felt compelled to do it. By the time I had finished cleaning and clearing I had reached the point of exhaustion.

The house ready, I invited Sonya, a friend from London, to stay, and at the same time my cousin Faith arrived with her two children. When she saw the state uncle was in she admonished me for not getting a psychic healer. As I had managed to successfully suppress all thought of anything psychic for nearly two decades, getting psychic healing for Uncle Frank had not crossed my mind. Faith called around and made the arrangements for my uncle to be visited by a psychic healer. When told this I got a feeling of dread so to avoid my meeting the healer I planned to go out with Sonya on the afternoon of the visit.

The day dawned and I had planned it carefully. It was 1pm and lunch over, I made my way down the hall to my room to get ready to leave with my friend. The healer was due at 2pm. I was halfway down the hall when I collapsed with what appeared to be a heart attack. I was 37 years old! The doctor's office was called but he was out making house calls. I understood he would not receive the message until late in the afternoon. An ambulance was also called. Surprisingly neither ever showed up.

It was nearly time for the healer to arrive and they didn't want her to find me in the hall. They felt they shouldn't really move me, but after much deliberation I was moved into my room and laid on the bed. Sonya elected to stay with me. I lay there in a stupor and heard the doorbell ring somewhere off in the distance. Later I learned from Faith what had transpired.

Gladys the healer arrived and was shown into the living room where Uncle Frank sat waiting. She reacted in surprise when she saw him, stating, "This is not my patient". She went on to say the patient she expected to see was female, accurately describing me and my room. Gladys said she had actually visited me during the previous night in an out-of-body experience and remembered every detail of the room. She had entered the room by stepping over the window ledge. She said she had wondered why my bed was in the center of the room and what the large object hanging from the ceiling was.

My room was on the front of the house. It had a wide bay window that reached from the ledge, which was only 18 inches from the floor, to just below the ceiling. This allowed a full view of Portreath bay and the harbor. It was a very large room and I had put my bed in the middle of the room to section off the space for living, painting, and writing. I had hung a bright orange trawler net across the ceiling and used it to keep my clothes in. There was no way she could have seen into the room before entering, as the curtains had been drawn when I was first taken in there.

Faith knew that if I was in my normal senses I would be furious with her, but because Gladys was so accurate with her details, she couldn't believe anything other than the *"Powers that Be"* had obviously taken over. Faith brought the healer in to see me.

I was in a terrible state still faintly blue from the struggle to breathe. A little foam was escaping from my mouth and Sonya was kindly wiping it away. As the healer approached she said, "Ah! There you are, we'll soon have you right". She was practically ripping off her coat as she hurried towards the bed and stood behind me. As she placed her hands on my forehead I had my first profound, all engulfing, internal Spiritual experience of Divine Light. The Light got brighter and brighter and just as I wondered if I could stand any more a Spirit Soul appeared way off in the distance that I realized I knew very well. At the same time without a word being spoken I became conscious that the reason for my being here on this planet at this time was to heal and to teach ancient spiritual truths. As I remembered, I groaned as my immediate reaction was that I did not want to know about any spiritual work, I was just too tired and the work I foresaw was eternal. When I later recalled the experience I assumed the soul I saw must be my master, for the Light shone so brightly all around him.

My uncle did receive healing that day, but in the future as we had both elected to continue with Gladys for healing, we drove across the peninsular to Falmouth.

At one of my sessions Gladys informed me that my guides had told her that the previous month of cleaning at my uncle's had been a preparation for my awakening. It was to aid release of things in my past. I was also informed that I had not only cleaned the house but had cleared the negative energies left behind by the women and their illnesses. The change in me was instantaneous and I was now ready to move on.

I received healing from Gladys during the five months that I stayed on. During the sessions, through Gladys, I received a lot of information. I learned that my uncle's mother-in-law had knitted the blankets. She would sit and knit, at the same time sending out bad thoughts to people. This negative energy went into the blankets, and I had been guided to take them on to clear them. I also learned that the clearing of the house was not only a physical exercise, but also a psychic one. The energies had needed changing. This had caused me to become exhausted on all levels of my being, physically, spiritually, psychically, emotionally and mentally, hence my collapse. This created the opportunity for my spiritual opening, and the return of my spiritual abilities.

I was different, and it took awhile for me to get used to feeling different, not to mention being psychically open again. I tried to put off the inevitable but found that my higher self had taken over. I could not control my healing experiences as I was thrown into situations where they were needed. Frequently, people instinctively knew that I could help them, and they would ask for healing. Soon I was choosing to work with the healing energies, and having the awakened knowledge within me, I found myself calling on my spirit guides for guidance.

I worked in this manner for the next four years, at the same time attending the Spiritualist Association of Great Britain's Headquarters in Belgrave Square, London to receive healing. The information that came through while giving or receiving healing I believed at the time to come from spirit, I later learned it to be knowledge from the depth of my own consciousness. This felt so comfortable and familiar.

During this period I also performed Soul rescue. I found that when I sat in my chair on returning home at night, I would automatically go into a deeper consciousness. My higher self had taken over. I would meet the souls of people who had passed over, but had never realized that they were dead. They were confused and lost and needed help to move on.

I did not change the way I lived. This involved writing music, painting and quite a lot of drinking, I just added healing, but more and more I was being pulled toward performing my healing service. I was reluctant to give up the life I was so familiar with and fought to keep it. Then I started to attend talks on meditation and things started to happen. Without intending to, I stopped smoking. One Tuesday evening I ran out of cigarettes and I never thought to buy any more. When I took a sip of my drink on the following Friday evening at the local pub, I found that I could not stand the taste. I stopped drinking. I realize the reason that I didn't have any withdrawal symptoms from these habits was because just hearing about meditation created an energy that was more satisfying. I had simply found something to take their place.

In 1974 I took meditation instruction. From that point things really changed. I stopped healing for a few months and concentrated on my meditation. Months later when people started approaching me for healing, people that didn't even know I was a healing channel, I started up again, but now I found that I was healing with a different intention. I no longer called in the guides but linked with the soul of the client. This was far more powerful and even allowed other life experiences to be dealt with quickly and without the client reliving any trauma. Over the next few years I became more and more involved in the practice of Healing.

In 1980 my partner David and I moved from London, England, to Bristol, a city in the West Country. This is when healing and teaching really started to take precedent over everything else in my life. I had decided at some level other than the conscious one to fulfill my mission.

THE HEALING EXPERIENCE

Within three months of moving into the house in Bristol my first clinic was operating and I began to see clients, some on a regular basis. My way of working had changed after starting to formally meditate and my intention of healing through spirit guides was a thing of the past. I simply forgot to tune in to them. Instead I now found that I was talking to the soul of the patient and I could only work with the intention of linking and working with that soul. I started to receive all sorts of information regarding the cause of the "disease" or life challenge in the form of impressions or pictures, including other-life experiences. The information was always attached to what was going on in the client's life at the time, so each session would be different. People came for many different reasons. Some came because they were depressed, maybe they would be at a crossroads in their life and were confused. Some came because they were physically ill. I saw people with arthritis, lung disease, spinal conditions, cancer, Bakkers disease, M.S. and of course heart disease. I even saw people that had brain damage and birth defects. The healing results varied, for it is the client's higher being that heals them when the time is right. Healers are needed as the medium for the channeling of the God force, universal energies.

Early in my healing, in fact while we still lived in London, I had an experience of Hodgkins disease disappearing the one time I saw the client. Another client attended for months while waiting to go to the hospital for treatment for her secondary cancer. When she went for the exam before admittance, they found no trace left of the tumor at all. There were clients whose physical condition did not change at all, but their attitude to life did. I have seen lives completely change direction sometimes from just one session.

During the healing session I would often get a vision of the lifetime that appeared to be the cause of the present complaint or situation. This very often is not what the client is looking for as he/she came with a conscious desire. This is an account of one such case.

Keith first came to see me after his wife and his girlfriend told him that I had suggested he could help sort out their triangle. I had been working with them for some considerable time and his soul experience had come up repeatedly with both of them in their individual sessions. Their experiences were so intertwined I felt it really needed his agreement, and his souls input, to clear the energies. I had formed an impression of a tall handsome and gentle man during the sessions with the two women, so I was not prepared for the man I answered the door to.

He was a stocky, strong looking man about 5'8". He had wire-framed glasses, rugged skin and disheveled red hair. Surely this was not the lover who had caused so much turmoil. He certainly did not fill my image of a Casanova. I noted that he had a hook where one of his hands should be.

As I sat listening to him I realized he was an intellectual and an artistic man who had overcome the fact that he had been born with only one arm. He enjoyed participant sports both on land and sea. He was exceptional at everything he did and I realized he was over compensating for his so-called 'disability'.

As I tuned into him I felt the anger in him that could have surfaced any minute and I immediately changed that energy so that I could get to a deeper level.

I was on a moor in the highlands of Scotland. A raging battle was in progress and I saw my client dressed in a kilt wielding a large sword. He was wild looking with his unkempt red hair, and was roaring as he slashed indiscriminately at all that came near him. Arms, even heads, were separated from their bodies and still he continued. He lived beyond that battle and felt no remorse during that lifetime. It was only after he had left his body in death himself that he realized what he had done. His actions not only affected the people he had maimed and killed, but also the circle of people that were attached to them.

It was then that his soul chose to reincarnate and experience living with a limb missing. He also knew that he would have to repay some of the folk he had deprived of their men. He handled it very well. Maybe a little too well, for now he was in the proverbial love triangle.

When the women had originally come to me the three of them, the wife, the girlfriend, and Keith, along with and the two children, had been sharing a cottage. The girlfriend left with her daughter and moved into her own house. The cottage was sold and he joined her in her home. His wife set up house with their son and her boyfriend. His relationship lasted, hers did not!

We will never know why he really came to me, maybe to get his deep seated anger released, but it did not help in solving the problem between the two women. There was a love-hate relationship between them still continuing seven years later when I left the country.

I do not presume that I have any of the answers, I can only relate what I have been given. With all the past experiences we bring into our present life and the clearing that has to be done of the energy of incomplete situations and relationships, it is no wonder that there are some people that appear to be fickle.

For a long time in our society we were inclined to think that to stay together in a relationship, no matter what, or to keep the same job, no matter what, was the correct thing to do. That thinking is changing, thank goodness! For to stay in a situation that has no challenge or love left in it is not conducive to one's growth.

Healing, because it works on all levels of consciousness, is not only known to remove energy blockages but also changes energy. This enables the soul to create new challenges, letting go of or using old situations necessary for new growth. At times the change is hardly noticeable, but there have been times when I have seen an immediate turn around in people's lives.

After a while I decided to record the sessions. This was so that the clients could go over the information whenever they felt a need. We found an added advantage. They would get the healing energies captured in the recording of the tape when they played them.

Each healing session was different. Sometimes the soul would call in spirit guides or whatever other energies necessary for the healing of the cause. This means that I have experienced Chinese, Tibetan, Japanese, Druid, French, Arab energies plus some energies that were not recognizable to me. I have also experienced the presence of Buddha, Jesus and many more bringing their energy to the healing room. As I continued seeing clients the sessions became quite an adventure for me. The instances when I received the information in the form of a vision were exciting, as I could then look in the history books to find out what was going on at that time. I used the style of dress to confirm the period involved. On the whole I have been successful in finding the approximate dates of the scene I have envisioned, but there have been some exciting experiences of times of which I could not find any record.

I recall one client who appeared to me as a primitive, complete with hairy body and long limbs. I felt his sense of panic as he scampered over rocks and through the dense vegetation.

Over time I came to realize that it was the energy acquired and brought away on passing from the body at death that was important from a lifetime, not who you had been. The energies were caused by the way the situations and interactions were handled. Imbalances in the energies were caused by any situations that had not been completed in that lifetime. This is not always the avoidance of completing. When a person dies suddenly, for example in an accident, or is murdered, there is no time for that person to deal with the situation and it is locked in to the energies that pass from the body. This will be dealt with when in an appropriate new body and time. The energy becomes cellular memory in the new body and affects the new personality. One such case follows.

Very tall, black and very elegant. Isabella was beautiful and seemed to be successful and self-assured. As I welcomed her I felt a sense of panic in her. I realized that I was tuning into another existence of hers, an experience of an incarnation when she was a white woman.

My inner sight saw that she was running through woodlands. Then my attention was drawn to a man who I instantly knew had set her cottage on fire. She was running away from the burning cottage with the man after her. She was dressed in the apparel of the seventeenth century. As she ran she kept tripping on the long skirt of her dress. The man was about forty years old and there was a feeling of evil about him. He was taller and ran faster so he was gaining on her. I knew that I was witnessing the last hours of her life. The fire quickly spread to the forest and her panic mounted as his hand reached out to grab her. He pulled her to the ground at the same time lashing out at her with his other fisted hand. Mercifully she lost consciousness as he vented his anger on her. When she regained consciousness her body was full of pain. Not daring to move for fear that her attacker was still around, Isabella lay there smelling the burning woods. Now panic took a new turn as she realized that she could not move and the fire was getting too close. Again she lost consciousness and this time did not regain it. She died as the fire cremated her body.

I related all this to Isabella as I was witnessing it, but she kept her composure and I received no indication at all whether this experience had affected her present life experience. I knew that she would have brought the energy of the fear of fire into this life with her. Maybe it had not shown itself yet.

During the actual healing session many different situations made themselves known that we needed to deal with. As each one came up Isabella would comment on how it had affected her life.

It wasn't until she was leaving that she mentioned the fire. She turned around at the door and said, "I have always, from very young, been afraid of – fire, I can even say the word now!" It was then that I realized that the fear was so great that this would not have been cleared by the experience of fire in this life, as she would have immediately left her body to avoid it. The only way to clear it was to have help in transmuting the energy, by healing it. It had been cleared as I was witnessing it.

As far as the fire energy was concerned I need not have completed the session with contact healing, but the healing helped her with current issues and she expressed to me how she enjoyed the feeling of peace it had left her with.

I came to realize that quite a few people prefer the glamour of locking into one of their other life personalities. It seems preferable to dealing with all of this lifetime's situations. I have met some of these souls in mental wards in England, and I have also met some that are living seemingly normal lives.

Recently I saw the energy of a man that in this life time was born into a family that cared for his every need, treating him like the Prince I saw he was in another life experience. The problem is that he feels that it is his right that everyone treat him in this way. He prefers to live locked in his Princely existence rather than this one, but at some point he will have to address these energies and take responsibility for his present life. His not taking responsibility for his current life as it truly is, and holding on to the out-moded energies of either this or any other lifetime is not healthy. It creates an imbalance and keeps him living in a world of illusion of his own making. Examining our own lives for this type of behavior is vital to our health and our continuing growth.

As I settled into working with the different clients, some progressed to the point of wanting to develop their own healing channel. I developed to the point of passing on what I knew. I started accepting individual students into the healing room to teach them, once I felt they were ready. Also I began to have people stay for weeklong healing experiences.

The next section will be about the journey that the soul takes in its quest to return to the source. Once a person is familiar with the concept that this particular life is but a blink in time, the making of decisions and the handling of life lessons become easier. To be familiar with knowledge of the path is essential as a base for the true reason for this book, which of course is Healing.

Margarite Westo

WHY ARE THERE TWO?

Why are there two?
What caused the split?
I look at the other
From where I sit.
I shut my eyes
The better to see,
That body of light
That used to be me.
To come to this world,
To be on this plane,
A soul must be trusting
Or what can it gain.
The prayers in the churches
Said under the dome,
Say Lighten our darkness,
Dear God, take me home.
I live in confusion
When following man,
Until desperation
Shows me God's plan.
A plan for the masses
Not just for the few,
To teach one another
To be Light anew.

Margarite

THE JOURNEY OF THE SOUL

My healing sessions combined with an inner knowledge and understanding gradually caused me to realize that there was a definite pattern to everyone's experiences. This I call the soul path or journey of the soul. I also received information through meditations and dreams. As a child I instinctively knew there was more to life than our conscious experience, but at that time I had no interest in questioning what. As my life involving other people took a turn toward more spiritual than psychic pursuits, the understanding came thick and fast. We all have a series of experiences we call incarnations. There is no set order to them, only that which we ourselves set by our need for growth. I have to delve into the fact that there is no such thing as linear time in the true state if I am to explain that all lives are being experienced at the same time. There is no past and no future, an impossible fact to grasp unless you have experienced the absence or stretching of linear time. Because everything is being experienced at the same time, it means that we can tap into any knowledge we need to aid us on our soul's journey.

To help the journey to be smoother, three laws must be observed.

(1) PHYSICAL HARMONY IN ONE'S SURROUNDINGS.

When you are not at harmony with your surroundings you are using too much energy in attempting to overcome incompatible vibrations. In this situation it is impossible to be living completely in one's own truth, and this is important. Often this causes a totally unconscious battle and shows in mood swings, ailments like flu, colds etc., or depression. We all have a different energy pattern. This explains why another's energy can be in harmony with these same surroundings. One can feel oppressed while all others around feel fine. Some people are in need of living in nature, some near water. To deprive the person of these energies can be the cause of disharmony.

The disharmony may even be caused by the energy of the actual ground a building stands on. Memories of past events linger until they are consciously cleared. There are so many different reasons for disharmony. Sometimes it is simply growth. You have outgrown the energies of the area. It doesn't seem to make any difference whether one practices meditation to create harmony or not; it is time to move on!

The energy of color plays a major role in the harmonizing of our lives. You will find that harmony with the color of your rooms and the overall color of the area is just as important.

(2) SPIRITUAL PURITY AND COMPLETE ISOLATION FROM IMPURE CURRENTS OF THOUGHTS

Thought does not stop in your head; it probably doesn't even start in your head. We are so influenced by the vibration of everyone else's thoughts, sometimes we get thoughts that are not ours. We then have to determine whether they are from, man, spirit, or our imagination. This of course works both ways and the vibration of our thoughts influences others as well. When we realize that thought is vibration, we can understand better the way it works.

Like attracts like, so if you have an impure thought, you are attracting other like vibrations to join with yours. For instance, angry thoughts attract other negative thoughts, creating a "Catch 22" situation until the anger is defused or released. This also applies when you have a pure thought of love or kindness; like attracts like. Keeping a pure channel will help you to evolve rapidly, as the magnetic light force is drawn toward you. The most difficult thing is to keep that pure channel while still living in the society of today. For instance, with so much violence it is hard to watch the news without having some thought of judgment or sympathy. There is an answer. When faced with the turmoil of the world one must keep one's energy centered. This does not mean a deep meditative state or one would not be able to function. Taking slow deep regular breaths will help to focus your energy and therefore transcend the energies of the situations you are faced with. Try it. You will be surprised to find that after a while it is automatic. Even the worst situations you are faced with will not have the same effect as they would have previously. We cannot change anything outside ourselves; therefore we have to change ourselves.

(3) EVOLVE THE STATES WITHIN, AND THE OUTER WILL TAKE CARE OF ITSELF.

We have two states to be concerned with, the body and the spirit. One way is to follow a balanced regimen of diet, physical activities, mental exercise, and meditation.

In addition to putting you in touch with your own spirit or higher self, meditation brings more oxygen to the body and calm to the nervous system. Over a period of time, this works on the cells, relieving stress so that your body has a chance to heal itself. A diet of natural foods, products of the earth, is not only for nutrition but for heightening your perception causing you to become aware of the now more frequent spiritual experiences. A sudden change in your diet can cause an imbalance in your energies and cause you to release toxins too rapidly; therefore it is wise to change your diet gradually. Red meat and associate products are the first items to eliminate, along with strong spices, caffeine, and alcohol while you introduce alternative foods such as grains, nuts, more vegetables, and herbs. Being in natural surroundings is very good for the soul. Go into the country, see and feel the beauty of creation, walk on the beach, go to the park, and meditate in the fresh air.

EVOLVING THE SENSES

As we travel along our soul path, we become more sensitive. The majority of humankind has evolved only five physical senses, whereas the perfect composite man has evolved seven physical senses and seven soul senses. As human beings our goal is to evolve to the point of mastery of the self and our individual destiny, though it is usually an unconscious one. Evolving both seven physical and seven spiritual senses is a way of helping us increase our ability to make the right choices.

I have to thank Zolar for the following comprehensive list of the senses we are working on to become adepts on the path of consciousness. It is from "The Encyclopaedia of Ancient and Forbidden Knowledge", published by Sphere Books Ltd of London England.

PHYSICAL SENSES	SOUL SENSES
1. **TOUCH**	The power to psychometrize; reading the energy absorbed by objects
2. **TASTE**	The power to absorb and enjoy the finer essence of the life wave.
3. **SMELL**	The power to distinguish the spiritual and psychic aromas of nature.

4. **SIGHT**	The lucid state of clairvoyance; seeing the non physical both objectively and internally with the third eye.
5. **HEARING**	The ability to perceive the ethereal vibrations termed clairaudience; the inner voices.
6. **INTUITION**	The capacity to receive true inspiration from the higher realms.
7. **THOUGHT TRANSFERENCE**	The power to converse with intelligence at will.

Once the human soul has attained the seven soul senses, it is the natural sequence that he/she will then be in conscious control of his/her life and therefore his/her destiny. The mind, rather than being in control as it was before the person attained the seven soul senses, has at this time come into line with the soul. Still the person retains the gift of choice as this is never taken away from a human being. A choice is now made at a deep level to become a helper to others. This could be in the form of a teacher, healer or guide. Many choose to stay in the background quietly living out their lives while their energy helps the many that come into contact with it in whatever way is necessary for them. At some point along the path, focus shifts from the material to the spiritual. It is then that true commitment to the spiritual path is made. Once committed the energy is fixed in the soul, and the soul takes over from the conscious mind and all decisions from that time on are made from a deeper level of understanding with less analyzing and more feeling. The choice has been made and there is no turning back, and once accepted on a conscious level, no desire to turn back. From this time on it is a matter of **allowing.**

At this time many children are growing up with their senses heightened. They are evolved souls that have incarnated to prepare themselves and others for the next step in the evolution of the planet. Also at this time, the most worldly adults find that they are becoming curious about psychic and or spiritual matters, or at least they have someone around them who is. The strength of the souls gathered here now will not allow the bigot or the persecutor to continue in the vein that they have followed for the past several generations. Times and the aura of the planet have changed, attracting more and more souls to explore and to work toward fulfilling their purpose.

Unfortunately, violence is in the cellular memory of many souls that have incarnated at this time. The soul requires the negative energies carried over from previous experiences to be cleared. This is done by the violent energy surfacing, attracting like energy creating situations to enable the person to face his/her shadow side. These situations touch the lives of souls who have no idea that they have incarnated at this particular time to experience and work through their choices. This unconsciousness causes many to blame others when problems arise in their lives. Blaming others creates prolonged suffering; this applies even when one blames oneself. When one accepts that the different situations that have to be dealt with are challenges rather than problems and takes responsibility for them, the act of dealing with each situation becomes easier and provides an opportunity for personal and spiritual growth.

GUIDANCE

ON FIRST MEETING MY GUIDE

I saw you again, Oh what comfort it brought
I didn't understand, I had thought you a dream,
Or had grown from my thought.
But this time I knew you were real
I was awake and felt you so near,
I WAS AWAKE, and there is nothing to fear.

Margarite

We all have spirit guides to help us on our way. One of these guides is a soul who has agreed to guide us throughout the lifetime and keep us on course, in spite of our spiritual amnesia. We have previously decided what it is that we need to do in this incarnation to enhance our overall growth. Whether it is to learn, to teach, or to serve in one of the many ways available to us, this guide is there to impress us with warnings of hazards on our path, encouraging us toward the goal that we have forgotten we set, even when we ignore him/her. We also have a guide who acts as a doorkeeper throughout the incarnation. This is to protect us from the many unseen entities that are trying to communicate with those left on earth and will use any channel they find open. During the course of a lifetime we are helped by many other guides. These guides have specific knowledge. When we become interested in a new subject we can draw to us a guide who has knowledge of that particular subject. This guide can inspire us and guide us toward a particular book or teacher, or put the information necessary directly into our consciousness. Most people never know these guides on the conscious level. This does not matter. What does matter is that we acknowledge the unseen help and protection we get and show our gratitude by following our own truth and by not allowing the world's standards to influence us.

Guides cannot live our life for us. We must learn to take full responsibility for ourselves and not rely on them. They will soon intervene in some way if we wander off course as we work through the many life lessons and tests we have to go through.

These lessons do not get easier as time goes on, even when one is following a path of meditation and love and has right intention. What does get easier is our ability to handle each situation as it arises. We learn that we have access to all of the intelligence of the Eons if we only remember to ask to receive. We also learn that we cannot afford to judge others, as we do not have the memory of the other's incarnations. It is probable that we have been in the same situation at some time during our journey, and that the situation touching another is in your life now as a test. We are all tested as we go through each incarnation.

Everything evolves in a spiral. Even plants emerging out of a seed unwind in a spiral. Metaphysically speaking the evolution of the soul is seen in a spiral. We cannot elevate to the next level of the spiral by anything other than our own effort and the growth it creates. At each stage we are prepared and helped by our guides and our masters; this may include being fed false information amongst all the wonderful guidance. We have to learn to live by our own truth. By feeding us the occasional piece of false information, our guides can teach us to feel and recognize the vibration of truth for ourselves. This is also a way to teach us the finer points of discrimination. If we are living totally in our own truth, we will not accept anything that we are not ready for. We will know! Once you have experienced the reaction in your body when you go against your own truth, you will try not to do it again, as it can be most unpleasant.

What is your own truth? It is a combination of the energy acquired from all of your previous experiences, including those that you have brought with you from other lives, both positive and negative. It is where you are on your own particular soul path. Your truth changes as you progress and release all of those energies and memories that were necessary to bring you to this point, but now no longer serve you. Your truth also changes as you acquire more spiritual understanding and become aware of and use more of your spiritual gifts. You are unique and cannot follow anyone else's way. We meet someone, we travel through life a while together sharing energies, learning, teaching and serving each other, then when we have all that we need from each other, we go on our way to share experiences with someone else, which hopefully leads to further growth.

If only we could understand this, the emotional pain that is experienced when parting with a loved one would be eased a little.

We would realize that our Higher Self is involved here and possibly even set up the situation. On this journey we meet souls we have known before, meet souls that we have never encountered before, and create situations that enable us to learn the particular life lesson necessary for our evolution toward the most beautiful goal of all, oneness with the Creator.

To close this section on a personal note, to reach that goal my daily intent is:

> *To feel that deep Divine Love more and more in my life,*
> *To know that whatever happens, even if I am going through the valley of the shadows,*
> *I am never alone and I am in the right place at the right time.*
> *Most of all to know that I am eternal and I am Love.*
> *This is a beautiful and wondrous thing.*

SOUL PATH CLEARING

Follow the One, avoid the many, be true to your inner light, and the mysteries of the invisible worlds will be revealed to you in the degree that you are ready and will use the knowledge thus attained in selfless service.

White Eagle

In 1975 my guides informed me that the method of healing that I was using was called Soul Path Clearing. Since that time many have completed the courses and are practiced in the use of this method of channeling healing. Instead of calling on the specific energy of any deity or master, we link with the soul. We then open the magnetic energy field, or aura, of the client. Once this is open, having linked with the soul, we read the energy presented to us. As we are receiving the information and passing it on to the client, any negative energy is being transmuted to positive energy. This occurs naturally as we act as the channel for the universal energy. In the majority of cases this eliminates the need for the client to go through the emotions of whatever is being released. Although the experience of this healing is subtle, it is deep and profound. I have seen people's lives change as they themselves find their old attitudes and beliefs changing, at times from just one Healing. Because of this change, it is necessary to counsel them so that they can better adapt to the changes happening in their life.

This is really fulfilling work and it is also fun for in linking with the soul, we experience many other lifetime scenes that were the cause of the trouble that has brought the client to Healing. These old situations and relationships have to be faced. If things were handled correctly at the time they were experienced, there would be nothing to throw us off balance later. When issues are not dealt with, at a later date something can act as a trigger to bring the old feelings or memories up to be faced once again. This trigger can be anything from a similar experience to a passage in a book, or even a word casually spoken within earshot. Now it is time to deal with the energies by releasing, accepting, or completing them; which always depends on the guidance of the soul.

When we meet someone who we feel we have known forever, we often mistake this for the opportunity to engage in a long-term relationship. Speaking generally, this meeting is only the need to complete with a soul that we have known before, but did not have the opportunity of saying goodbye. Hence the familiar feeling. Taking on a relationship instead of completing leads to even more to deal with at a later date as more karma is accumulated.

Soul-path healing is extremely helpful in all cases working at a deep level bringing in the correct energies necessary to help the process the soul has created.

Soul path healing can also be done at a distance. I was first prompted to use this distant method of healing in 1980 and was told to call it **Transfer Healing**. This manner of healing is sometimes more powerful than the contact or hands-on-healing. There are two reasons the soul allows the client to open to a deeper level. First, they are in the privacy of their own home; instinctively we let down our defenses when we are at home. Second, there is no need to revert to their 'normal' state to enable them to travel after the session. The reason we call it transfer rather than distant is because we either transfer the etheric body of the client to us to work on, or our etheric body travels to them. A transfer session can leave you feeling as though you have been in a deep, peaceful sleep, one you wish to stay in. I have received some extraordinary feedback from people that have had transfer healing. The following is how I came to perform transfer healing.

Gerald, a friend practicing cranial oesteopathy at a health spa in England, called me to tell me about his sister-in-law. His niece had called him and he thought the problem was an ovarian cyst. Because I channeled healing he had the idea that I could help her. Up to this time I did absent healing by prayer, or reading out the persons name in a healing circle that I led. That night as I lay down to sleep, the lady in Wales immediately popped into my thoughts. I saw her as a short round shape and found myself placing her on a conveyor belt. As the shadow of her body passed slowly in front of me I saw and felt what was wrong with each section. At her head was a big black cloud. I then felt the pain in her heart. Next I saw an extremely large black mass surrounding her navel. I was aware that her spine was very painful as well. What I could not see was an ovarian cyst. The next day Gerald called me and I told him what I had found. I said I must have been wrong, and we left it that he would get his niece to call me. When she called I repeated all that I had told Gerald, again stating that I must be wrong as I couldn't find any ovarian cyst. It turned out we were equally amazed at the session. Her mother had never had an ovarian cyst, she couldn't imagine where Gerald had got that from. Her mother had been in a depression for about two years, this explained the black cloud. She had suffered with heart trouble for years, that explained the pain I felt in the heart area and she had been going to a chiropractor for years to align her spine after an accident. The mass around her navel, well, this was what she had called to tell her uncle about in the first place. It was an inoperable tumor and she was in extreme pain and they gave her only a few weeks to live.

That night I was guided to send another healing but this time I went into the healing room and lay down on the healing couch. As I closed my eyes I immediately saw myself placing my hands on her shoulders and asked her soul for direction. There was no black cloud there and the pain had gone from her heart. I was not aware of her spine at all but I again saw the mass around her navel. It had not changed. I went deeper and then I was closing her aura. My eyes opened and I found I had been there thirty minutes. The next day the woman's daughter called me again. She seemed very excited. She had gone in to visit her mother the evening before and her mother was sitting up looking cheerful and told her she was free of the pain in her back, felt no discomfort around her heart and was not depressed anymore. The doctors could not explain this complete change in their patient. She had been on drugs for the pain, never seeming to get enough of them, and now did not want to take them at all. The cancer did not get cured, but as she had no pain the doctors could see no point in keeping her in the hospital. She spent the next two weeks happy at home surrounded by all her family and passed peacefully in her sleep having said goodbye to everyone.

It was this very different experience of healing that prompted me to ask my guides what to call it. From that time on I found that I was prompted to channel transfer healing more often than not and had continued to be amazed at the results.

Not long after moving to Bristol, I received a call from a lady with very advanced rheumatoid arthritis. Her sister had suggested she ask me for a healing to help with the pain. She explained that she was confined to a wheelchair and her hands were also very crippled. She lived the other side of England from me but wished me to visit to give her a healing. I explained that it was really too far for me to come, and asked if she would accept a transfer. I explained to the best of my ability how it worked. She said she would try it as she had nothing to lose. After instructing her how to prepare for the healing, I found myself telling her she must follow any impulses she got. I thought this strange as I usually told people to just lay there and enjoy the energy allowing the feeling of sinking into the bed. I prepared as usual and lay down. It was the thirty minutes that I had become used to. Before the day was out I had a call from the sister to tell me this remarkable story. Her sister, my client, had been put on the bed by the companion she lived with. She lay on top of the bed surrounded by cushions so that she would not fall off. All was quiet and she asked for healing through Margarite. In no time she felt energy move in her body and had the urge to get off the bed. Somehow she managed to squirm until she was on the side of the bed, with an effort she pushed herself to the floor. Her instinct told her to throw her arms around in the air and at the same time she was kicking her legs. She shook her hands and at the end of the thirty minutes she lay there exhausted. Her companion came in and was concerned until she saw the lady's body. It had straightened itself out.

I was so thrilled for this lady and surprised at her remarkable recovery that I occasionally called to see how she was doing. Eight years later, when I was about to leave England to move to the United States, I learned that she had either bought or inherited a cottage in Ireland and was living there taking in and caring for stray animals.

Each one of us has a lot of old energies to clear and we each do it in our own way. The soul tries to attract our attention in whatever way it deems necessary. First there is a hint, but if the hint is ignored the soul creates another more definite situation to catch the attention. This is rather like a parent trying to get a response from a child. The child is engrossed in a game or a book and either doesn't hear or chooses to ignore the parent. The parent first speaks normally, then shouts, then if the child does not respond, finally clips the child round the ear as a way to gain his attention. I personally had many hints over the years and finally my soul put me in a position that I could not ignore.

Margarite Westo

MY OWN BATTLE WITH ILLNESS

From the beginning of my life one thing or another was wrong with my body. It started with bronchial pneumonia when I was a baby, after which I had a yearly dose of bronchitis. This finally ended with the bout of bronchitis while I was giving birth to my son when I was nineteen.

I remember when I was quite small being pushed in a chair in the hospital to have acid applied to the warts that covered the bottom of my feet. At boarding school I was continually getting crops of boils first in one ear, then as they healed up, in the other. I was kept isolated at these times to prevent getting a "draft in my ears", which would be caused by the other girls opening and shutting the door. It was one minor thing after another restricting my involvement in both indoor and outdoor activities.

When I was fourteen the accidents started. I have had thirteen in all – as if I was trying to experience as many forms of accident as I could. These included being involved in two major car accidents, one of which required plastic surgery to my face. Others included a boating accident on the River Thames in England, a cycling accident while in a mass start race, then another cycling accident while filming as an extra in a movie entitled 'Poets Pub' on location from Pinewood Studios. I had a very bad shock that knocked me unconscious and threw me across the room when I was turning off the television; I have fallen out of the high cab of a truck while it was moving! Needless to say these accidents have caused my body to act up over the years but I found it too painful to dwell on the doctors prognosis so I ignored it and lived my life as though everything in my body was normal. Now I realize that my attitude stood me in good stead and I would not be as healthy as I am today had it not been for that attitude. Attitude, when combined with spiritual or energy healing, is especially powerful in the healing process and rebuilding of a body.

Through my teenage years I had digestive problems, then in my early twenties I started having yearly operations caused by a mistake the hospital made during the birth of my child. In my late twenties the build up of suppressed emotions from my experiences became too much and I had a nervous breakdown. It was the late fifties and the time when the early experiments to see whether people could be treated without drugs was going on. I was fortunate in having an open-minded doctor who was also a family friend who decided I would be a good candidate. I spent five months as a voluntary patient in a group therapy unit rather than a hospital.

In my thirties the problems continued and I was thirty-seven years old when I had what appeared to be a heart attack. (See My Awakening) It was then that I first experienced *psychic healing*, and at the same time discovered that I had a specific task that I had not been fulfilling. I have been informed by my guides that this avoidance of the task led to my illnesses etc.

I had visited nearly every department of the Middlesex Hospital in London, England. One after the other my different organs, joints, bones, glands, and my nervous system were affected for some unknown reason. Each part of me was under a different specialist each having a morning clinic. One night I had a bad time getting to sleep because of the discomfort of a skin allergy. This caused me to sleep in late the next morning. It happened that I was due at one of the clinics for a test and arrived just as it closed for the day. I caught the doctor and nurse as they were locking up and explained that I had over slept. The doctor became impatient with me telling me I should go to bed earlier at night. My nerves were so shot that I lost the composure that I was trying so hard to keep. I burst out crying and after questioning me further the doctor decided to send me to the out-patient department for a series of tests to see what was going on. After a while I was told that I had a thyroid condition and was treated accordingly. This was correct, but not the whole picture. I improved sufficiently to get a job and went to work for a large international corporation in one of their offices.

After a couple of years I was finding it more and more difficult to get to the office. Some days I would arrive in tears from the stress of the journey on the subway and the increasingly painful walk from the station. My boss sent me down to see the company doctor. He actually listened to me as I answered his questions. This was something that I had not experienced in another doctor, they seemed always preoccupied doing two things at once during my visits. The company doctor sent me back to the Middlesex hospital, but this time to a friend of his and with a letter. I don't know what the letter said, but the doctor took a lot more tests and eventually I was called back to receive the results. I had a rare form of arthritis, an S.L.E. disease called Poly Arteritis Nodosa. He would not tell me what it involved but told me to get in touch with the arthritis association for details. He said he would see me again after I had digested the information about the disease.

I was sent all sorts of information. I recognized they could have been relating to my life from the age of twenty-three when my first symptom appeared. After twenty-one years of misdiagnosis, including being thought a malingerer and having a mental condition called Psychogenic hysteria, a cause had been found for my many physical challenges. Unfortunately there was no known cure, and no way to stop the deterioration of my body. The only thing the medical profession offered me was drugs to control the pain. This I decided I did not want and instead I did breathing exercises and meditation from which I found some relief as it relaxed me. At first I felt desperate and went through a period of depression. Then I went through the process of accepting and buying into the doctor's diagnoses and prognosis; adjusting my life accordingly.

In England when you are officially classified as disabled, you are assigned to a welfare officer who looks after your interests and makes sure that you have all the necessary aids for your comfort. At the time the doctor diagnosed me he also gave me a letter for the health department to allow me to get permanent disablement benefits. When I moved my case was assigned to a new welfare officer who had also just moved to a new area. He called to make an appointment to meet me to see if I was receiving all the care that I was due. I tried to explain that although I had a car, I could only walk a few steps before my body went into spasm from the pain. As it would be both painful and stressful for me to come to his office I asked if he could come to my apartment. He insisted that I see him at his office and being fearful of losing my benefits, I agreed. Driving my car was the thing I liked best at this point. The driving seat was comfortable, and the speed gave me a sense of freedom after the painful struggle to walk. The problem was getting to the car. I had a wheelchair, but needed someone to push it.

The neighbors were very kind helping me out of the car and into the apartment, but in the daytime it was a long wait as they were either at work or school. I had been given two walking sticks rather than crutches as my joints were so bad I couldn't stand anything under my arms.

When the day arrived, I got myself to the car and drove to my appointment. By the time I reached the Welfare Officer's desk I could barely move as my body had become a sheet of pain. I couldn't believe my ears as the welfare officer castigated me for not explaining to him how bad I was. He said he would have come to see me at home if he had realized. What could I do? I knew that I had tried: he just hadn't heard.

When I left the office he didn't offer to help me, so I slowly made my way back to my car which was parked immediately outside by the curb. I reached the gate. Now all I had to do was cross about four feet of sidewalk. I put out one of my walking sticks so the people rushing by would notice that I needed space to cross to my car; but I was ignored. I waited and waited with the stress and pain building up. I was practically yelling for help by the time I was allowed a gap to get through. The people were so wrapped up in their own thoughts that they were oblivious to anything going on around them. I got very angry, not because they did not help me, but because they were so unaware that they had legs that worked. I wanted to yell at them, "You can walk, you can walk!" Instead I kept my painful feelings locked up until I was alone in my car. I drove home and parked outside my building. Then exhausted I let go to uncontrollable crying. I was there for over an hour before a neighbor came home and helped me inside.

For three days, I was in a state of intense emotional venting: cursing everything in the universe including God, and crying because I had done so. I started not only praying but screaming for help, not just to relieve the pain but also to remove this life draining illness from my body.

In the end, this horrendous experience turned out to be a blessing in disguise. I had needed a powerful experience to shake me out of my apathy and bring my anger to the surface to be vented. I had reached the turning point. I now refused to accept the doctor's prognosis. I did not deny my illness, I did not give it permission to exist!

MY HEALING

With this new attitude my prayers were more focused on asking for help and to be shown the way. The guidance was immediate and I was shown the method of breathing and self-healing that I use and teach to this day. Then a few days later while out getting my groceries, I was drawn to talk to a complete stranger who then was kind enough to help me back to my car. We sat in my car and talked for over an hour. It turned out that Joan was a psychic healer. She and her husband Charles ran a healing clinic in town. During the course of the conversation Joan asked me if I would like her to come round sometime and give me a healing. I agreed immediately, I knew I could do with all the help I could get. So I began to receive healing from her. When the pain got too bad for me to deal with, I would scream at God in the morning for help. At precisely one o'clock on these days Joan would call me to offer to come around to give me a healing. It never failed. I never needed a telephone to call her! She seemed to be on my line to God.

I had stopped visiting the Spiritualist Association of Great Britain as the journey had become too stressful. My body became even more painful as I went through a healing crisis. Many strange energies and memories came to the surface to be released during this time of process, and I somehow knew deep within me that I would eventually be well and did eventually get well enough to start traveling to Belgrave Square for regular healing once again.

The association has a whole floor dedicated to healing. The healers form groups, each group has a leader. When I first went I had an interview with one of the leaders and she assigned a healer to me. Once you start with a healer you continue seeing the same one. This healer keeps a record of your visits and your progress. My healer was David Biggs who gave up one afternoon a week from his job to serve in the way he was gifted.

On returning to receive healing after so long I was happy to find David still there and remembering me, and so I resumed my weekly visit to Belgrave Square. One particular Wednesday afternoon, I was disappointed to find David absent, but having struggled to come so far, I decided to stay and see another healer from the same group. This lady knew nothing about me and did not have access to David's reports. As she channeled the healing I saw a large hand cover hers and told her so. At that time she did not reply. In fact, unlike David, she was silent throughout the whole healing. After she had completed the session she said that a very powerful healing guide had been with us. After she had written the report he asked her to get me to spell out the name of the disease. I did so and later realized that the reason that I had to spell it out was to imprint that particular day on my mind as the day that the disease was eliminated from my body. It turned out she had written arthritis instead of arteritis. Over the next few years I had several blood tests ordered by different doctors who would not believe the disease had gone. As there was no trace of the disease they believed it was in remission. It has never returned.

My body had deteriorated, and now the damage had to be repaired. X-rays showed the cartilage in my joints had been eaten away, and I knew my organs were not functioning properly anymore. My nervous system was shot, and the pain this caused was really unbearable. My hearing and sight had also been affected.

By the time the doctor at the Middlesex hospital diagnosed my disease, I had been channeling healing for others for eight years. It was sometime before I realized that the act of healing others brought my own needs to the surface more quickly, and I had a lot to heal with all my past accidents, illnesses and emotional upsets.

Joan continued to come around to give me healing, and I tried never to miss my visits to David, my healer, for they were very exciting. David's healing not only helped to relieve the pain, but I regularly received what I now know were spiritual visions during my sessions. My healer was also psychic, and I received information about both my past spiritual activities and my future service. During this time I continued my healing of others, and I noticed that the more I opened as a channel for others, the more I seemed to get better myself.

I had been trained by my entertainer father to hide any negative feelings and never let anyone see that I was anything but joyful and happy. This resulted in my having a great deal of suppressed anger and hurt. Spiritual healing was instrumental in releasing this pain, and in bringing these emotions to the surface. Each week yet another situation or emotional trauma would surface to be dealt with. Between sessions I was having incredible dreams and daytime visions. I would experience unfamiliar feelings as I processed at a level of my consciousness that I could not interfere with.

I can never thank my healer David Biggs enough for being such a clear and non-judgmental channel. David was the one who first started me wondering about the soul and the soul path.

As with all life's challenges this major illness turned out to be a blessing in disguise, for during the course of my own healing I became more familiar with my soul and it's path. Since that time so much has happened in my life. I am no longer that same person who first went to the healer.

You know, if you ask you receive, and at last I knew what to ask!

WHAT DO I MEAN BY SELF?

During a deep meditation I experienced the separation of the physical body, the mental body (mind), the emotional body (feelings), and the spiritual body (soul or spirit). I will explain these separate bodies later. In another meditation I experienced the complete Oneness of these "bodies". In yet another meditation I was shown my own immortality. I realized I was outside of my body looking at myself sitting there meditating; then I was outside my body looking at myself sitting there meditating. This was repeated over and over again, like being in a hall of mirrors. Thousands of me watching me, going off to the ends of the universe until I appeared as a mere speck in the far distance, each of these images identical. The feeling that I received from this experience was so incredible. I knew that nothing could ever hurt me again, in fact nothing had ever hurt me! I was living an illusion and I had just experienced reality. From this I also realized that the core self is energy and that everything we do externally affects the energetic evolvement of the core self.

Before these meditation experiences made me aware, I cared only for my physical body, and not very well! When someone said to me "Look after yourself", it never occurred to me that I had to be aware of the energies I mixed with, I thought it meant physically safe! I was never taught science of any kind at any of the schools I attended, so I had never considered any of this. I had avoided anything I judged to be of a serious nature, being more interested in music and what I then thought was having a good time. The concept that the energy of places we frequent can affect how we feel emotionally, and physically, would have seemed to me to be more science fiction than universal truth. I had to come to my own realization, and this I did by experiencing this truth over and over again until I got it. I now realized that I could protect myself by being more discriminating about whom I mixed with and where I went. I would now choose which energies I would allow to influence mine. Feeling out the energies has taken some practice, but eventually come to be automatic.

To me self is energy, a combination of all that you are and all that you have experienced on your soul's journey, and the purpose of incarnating is to evolve the self.

ENERGY

Everything originally was, is, and will always be, energy. This energy can be seen surrounding everything by those who train themselves to see beyond the solid forms. The scientists call this energy <u>the magnetic field.</u> Metaphysicians call it the <u>aura.</u> The state of mental or physical health can be observed through the aura. Moods show up, as does thought. In fact, we can easily be read through the aura by a developed psychic or a seer.

For years I experienced mood swings. At the time I put them down to my poor physical condition. On waking in the morning I found I either felt good and the day got progressively better, or I felt down and I could do nothing but get depressed, and emotional, until I finally went to sleep. Usually the next day I would be back to feeling good again. I suffered for a considerable time before I realized that it was my own energy attracting like energies to it, just as a magnet would. I found that if I, for whatever reason, thought of a painful experience, usually in a past relationship, I felt a dread in the pit of my stomach and my energy level immediately dropped and I would feel depressed.

This happened even though to the observer I was happy and OK with whatever we were talking about. I found I also had a similar energy experience when I was with certain people, although there was no animosity between us.

What do you do to desensitize a magnet? You rub it on some material that is not metal. I decided to test this out with my magnetic energy field. I would breathe deeply and slowly and imagine rubbing myself with Light. When in the shower, I would imagine that the water was Light and even extended this imagery to the food I ate and the beverages I drank. It's amazing how when you put on a light, darkness disappears! None of these exercises would have been necessary if I had caught and changed any negative thought I had when it first presented itself.

The healing of the self is achieved through a combination of awareness, disciplines, and practices. The most important of these is learning to quiet the mind and connect with the inner self, which can be done in many ways. Some find listening to harmonious classical music beneficial; others like to take a solitary walk. I find meditation to be the way for me. There are many teachers and methods to guide you into meditation and the correct teacher or way is purely a matter of individual choice. Once a method is chosen there are two important things that it is advantageous to follow.

1. Create a special meditation area where you feel quiet and comfortable.
2. Put aside time to practice.

The correct diet is very important for our energy. Each of us, although we appear to be the same, has a slightly different chemical makeup, we need the energy of the food we consume to be compatible with our energy, and with the energy of other foods eaten at the same meal. This helps us to keep in balance and therefore healthy.

Becoming aware of the energy of people with whom we spend time is most important to our well-being. We interact with other energy at work, at home, and at play. Have you noticed how either exhilarated or drained you have felt after a visit with certain people? How a visit to the hospital also leaves you drained or realized that although you wished to see the friend or loved one, you would rather have not had to go?

Our energy is ever changing without our recognizing it. How you will feel at any given time depends on what you have allowed into your energy field. Stay aware. Many of us have had those feelings of dread when we have agreed to see someone we really didn't want to see, or go somewhere we really didn't want to go. That is your instinct sending you a message through your body. The energies would not be compatible for you. So in future, think twice before accepting an invitation, or should I say 'feel'?

Practice going within and learn to distinguish between the inner guidance and the mind. This guidance will help with every aspect of your daily life if you take the time to practice and then "listen" to your body.

CLEANSING OUR ENERGY

As stated earlier, the aura is the magnetic energy field that surrounds living things. The aura shows exactly what state we are in. It extends from the human body and can be any size from a few inches, which is very close to the body, to a couple of miles, as in the case of a spiritual master when administering to his devotees. Each person controls his aura by the energy that he takes on board and the energy he gives out.

A person's aura varies according to what they are doing or thinking. For example, an individual in a state of fear keeps the aura wrapped closely to the body for protection, while one who is in a state of giving has the aura open and extended.

While evolved souls generally have conscious control of their auras, this is not the case for everyone. Unaware and not so evolved souls sometimes leave their auras wide open and are apt to pick up a variety of energies, both positive and negative. If not cleared in some way, these negative energies can become harmful over a period of time. The cleansing of the aura on a regular basis helps to keep us more in balance and healthier.

Taking a shower not only cleanses the body but also cleanses the aura. Water is one of the purifiers on this planet and perfect for cleansing auras. Those who still feel dirty after a shower might consider taking a swim, and allow themselves the luxury of dunking under the water. I always feel invigorated after a swim and I know it is because I have allowed my energy field to be submerged and so be completely cleansed.

Cleansing the aura energetically is very important. Many people actually feel physically lighter afterwards. Receiving a healing is a good method to do this as it also balances the chakra or energy points, helps remove blockages, and promotes spiritual growth.

The main thing is stay aware. When aware it is easier to stay in balance or at the least to know when to clear yourself.

Everything I have mentioned is of equal importance in maintaining a well-balanced life. If you follow these guidelines, you will be rewarded with not only good health but also a sense of achievement.

Margarite Westo

CLEARING LAND AND BUILDINGS

In the first chapter I mentioned Gladys the psychic healer telling me that I had cleared the negative energies from my uncle's house in Portreath. I did not really understand this at the time although I felt good when she told me. Since then I have had innumerable experiences where I have been directed to clear or change energies.

I was going through a period when I was super sensitive to the vibrations of people when in public. At least at the time I assumed it was the people. It was when on vacation in the West Country of England that I realized that it could be the actual building.

It was approaching lunchtime and we looked for a place to stop. We reached a village and found a very old and attractive inn. Inside it was delightful with its big fireplace and highly polished tables. Copper and brass ornaments were placed here and there, and tankards hung in a row behind the bar. The place appeared deserted so we sat down to wait for the barkeep to appear.

It was when we sat down that I started to feel the pressure building up in my head, and it couldn't have been more than a few minutes before I couldn't stand it and hurriedly left to wait in the car. As I waited I knew without a doubt that it was the energy of the building I was feeling, the energy inside that pub was very old and very heavy. I concentrated on releasing the energy and after a short while I felt like myself again. I didn't know I could clear the energies of a building, so didn't even try. I was learning one step at a time!

One day my husband decided to take a look at an area that the county of Somerset had designated as a nature reserve for the sake of the school children and their teachers. It was a pleasant drive on a beautiful day. We were both interested in photography so once there we went to see what we could find in the way of wildflowers and butterflies.

As we were following a dirt trail I became aware of a battle scene. I felt compelled to drop to the ground and related what I was seeing. I knew that I had to clear the ground and found it happening without any conscious effort on my part. I did not feel any souls trapped on this ground and what came to me was that I was tapping in to memories that were held in the ground. It was through this experience that I knew how to deal with the energy of memory.

Years later I had another learning experience when I was called on to clear an office building in one of the northern states in the USA. They had been having several negative experiences that could not be explained. It turned out to be a multi story building built on a small hillock.

I arrived early and sat in my car at the back of the car park to prepare myself after the journey. As I centered my energy I noticed that there were two spirit guardians on the land. This puzzled me as I had been led to believe that the guardian of a particular area of land left when handing over to a new one, but it was uncommon for the guardian to change. One of the guardians I recognized as an American Indian, but the other one appeared to be very ancient and I had no idea about him at all. I tried to communicate with them but found it impossible until I approached them one at a time. I realized that they did not communicate with each other. I learned that day that America had been inhabited long before the tribes emigrated here, but more importantly that levels of the previous energy can still exist when new civilizations have taken over.

Here's the story.

The ancient one said this is sacred land and the Indians had defiled it when they took it for their own without asking permission from the ancient ones, the gods. The American Indian said that the land was sacred to them and that the white man had taken the land without asking permission from the Great White Spirit and the energy that this was creating was not what this land was for. I related this to the people that came to the talk that I gave before I performed the clearing and we sent prayers and requests to the appropriate spirits. When I went from office to office, I came across one where I got the strong message that whoever was using that office was working with money as his priority, and that greed would not be tolerated. I wondered if this was the energy the guardian had meant. I completed all that I could do that day, but as is usual for me I found myself mentally go back to the building and repeat the clearing for a period of time.

Clearing is not always the most pleasant or interesting task. One client called me to clear his house, cars, and business. He had been a very wealthy man running his own factory with a happy marriage and well balanced and loving children. I began by sitting in his living room and centering my energy. He hadn't confided in me what was happening in his life other than his failing business, but he didn't seem like a man who would request a clearing for that.

The first impression I got was of a snake and slowly I tuned to chanting in a monotone. I saw that dark energy was being directed at the house and immediately created extra protection for myself. I felt that the energy was coming from someone wishing my client harm most probably in retaliation for something he/she thought had been unfair. It didn't matter whether the cause was real or imaginary, the thoughts reached their target and the results were the same. Negative energy was born that worked in the same manner as an intentional spell would, and yes, it could have been a spell. It created negativity in my client's energy field that attracted more and more negative situations and events to occur in his life. Magnetic energy, like attracts like!

After I had completed the clearing and cut the links to whoever was the instigator I told the client what I had found. He opened up to me.

It seemed he had found it necessary to fire one of his Cuban employees because of some sort of misconduct. He didn't go into what the misconduct was, but he did tell me that he had not had cause to fire anyone before and it had not sat well with him. He had recently realized that it wasn't long after firing the man that he started to experience bad luck, his children started acting up, and his marriage started to break down. His business was failing and from being a very wealthy man he was now attempting to keep his head above water. This had taken less than two years. He told me he was now wondering whether he was the cause of everything going wrong in his life as he had learned that feelings of guilt caused negative energy. It seemed that this had turned out to be a catch twenty-two situation and to stop his negative energy recreating the old pattern I needed to channel a healing for him.

When performing clearings of this sort I sometimes get bombarded with dark energy and when this occurs it takes a lot of strength to either transmute it or send it to light. There is often a lot of resistance and even though I am a channel it is at these times that I end up physically tired.

There was a time when I wondered why some people were directed to me for healing. If there was a reason at the time it confused me, but very often there wasn't one. I knew some people came out of curiosity, but the others! It took a few years to realize that everything was in Divine order, and I would be using the links I had made with them to take me on to somewhere else that the work was needed.

MAKING THOSE ENERGETIC CONNECTIONS

I first met June when she came to the Sylvan center to volunteer her services and those of her children. I put them to work outside with Pat one of my probationer healers. When it was time for me to take a break I went looking for them to see if they would like me to show them some of the grounds. I decided to take them to an area where we had already cleared the path and steps down the mountainside. Growing both sides were enormous Rhododendron bushes in full bloom. These shrubs had been brought from the Himalayas and planted around 1900 by Flora the lady who at that time owned Sylvan. The shapes of the petals and the colors were unusual and magnificent and I knew they would enjoy viewing them.

As we made our way down the steps I suddenly got such a strong message for June. I knew nothing about her at that point except where she lived. I had assumed that she was married as she had three children with her, but I found myself telling her that she was going meet an old boyfriend of hers from a long time ago and that she would marry him. June was surprised and told me she came from the area but had lived abroad for many years with her husband. They had recently been divorced and she had come home and was staying with her family. A few days later she called me to say she had been to the hospital to visit the mother of a man that she had not seen since they were young. They had been engaged but they had broken it and they had both married someone else. He worked abroad and had only just arrived for a short visit to see his mother. They renewed their relationship and it wasn't long before they were married and left the area.

Over the time June came to the center we got friendly and she told me more of her life. June had married an Arab diplomat and they had these three children. They moved to the countries he was assigned to one of them being Uganda. At that time Idi Armin was in power. It was normal for June's husband to drive the children to their school but this particular morning it just so happened that June drove them. As she drove out of the gate they were ambushed and she was dragged from the car and violently slashed with a machete.

Leaving her for dead, Armin's men took off. Of course she survived, and considering what the children must have witnessed and the fear that they must have felt they appeared to me to be really well balanced.

Years later a client of mine in New York rented an office in Midtown Manhattan. She called me to clear the old energies out for her before moving her business.

As I prepared myself I started to feel a strange reluctance to do the work. In spite of this I knew I would be all right once the clearing started. I linked with the address of the property and was aware of the darkness there. As I worked to clear it I couldn't help wondering how this could have become so devoid of light. I completed the work and closed impatient to ask my client about the previous tenants. To my surprise it had been the office of one of Idi Armin's government officials.

It struck me that it was not coincidence that I had been given this task after dealing with what June had related to me and the prayers I had said for all concerned in the attack at that time. I had made the connection! I was surprised that I was working on the energy of a distant land and assumed I must be one of many.

When I was working in the office in down town Manhattan, I had a young man come for healing for a damaged leg. During his visits we would talk and he told me that his aim was to work with a designer, preferably a shoe designer. He stopped coming and sometime later I got a call from Germany. He asked me if I would be willing to work with his boss, a female designer. I congratulated him on fulfilling his ambition and told him I would be delighted to work with her. I informed him that she would have to get in touch with me herself. This she did explaining that she was experiencing a lot of nightmares and it had resulted in her feeling depressed and a dread to go the office. I told her that it sounded like there was something to clear either from her energy or maybe the building and I would work with her for as long as it took to get her back to feeling comfortable again.

I prepared myself for the first session. As I tuned in and linked with my new client the visions came thick and fast. With them came a feeling of horror, and I could hear a jumble of voices shouting although I could not understand what was being said. I felt the energy of war. If this was what she was experiencing it was no wonder she was feeling so bad. A highly polished jackboot came into my consciousness then a row of them marching in goose step. This told me I was tuning in to the Second World War. I knew my client had not been born at that time so made a mental note to ask her if any of her family had been involved. It turned out that none of her family had served in any part of the military that would have marched so what I was working with remained a mystery.

I continued to have extreme visions and there was always a jackboot somewhere in each session. I worked with her sister and her father but the boots did not show up there. We were in communication a lot but no explanation surfaced.

One day the young man who had introduced us called to ask my input on moving with his boss to a different town. I did not know that she had decided to move, and I asked what had made her come to that decision. It seemed that business had not been too good since her focus had been elsewhere and she wanted to make a fresh start. I asked him how he felt about moving; surely he had got used to being in that part of Germany and had settled into his apartment. He told me he had bought a bicycle to get around and riding it around town had shown him how different Germany was to the USA. You only had to have the wheel a fraction over the line at a light to be in trouble. Everything was so tight. I realized I had never asked where they were and where they were thinking of moving the business to. He didn't know where she was thinking of going to, but now they were in Munich. He said at least if they moved they would be getting out of that building. Something clicked inside me and I realized that any thoughts of the building had been completely erased from my mind ever since starting to work with her. I asked what was wrong with the building. He said it had a terrible vibe. I asked him to tell me about it. That was when I found out that the building had been the head quarters of the S.S in the second-world-war and part of it had been used for interrogation and torture.

I momentarily wondered how such a strong vibration had not penetrated the healing sessions, then I realized that it must have been blocked so that I would continue with the clearing without getting involved. I completed with a clearing on the building linked through the young man.

As far as I know she did move to another town and I believe he went with her. All three of us were used to serve in this case and for myself I felt it was a wonderful way to be used as a channel!

Margarite Westo

THE MENTAL BODY

As we breathe, so we take in sustaining energy with each breath. The energy at this time is pure. The thought we have in our mind, and the mood we are in at the time, receives that sustaining energy empowering them. Therefore it is imperative that we are aware of our thoughts and moods not allowing them to run uncontrolled. For instance, when we are in a negative mood, the energy will feed the thought and enhance our negativity, so change that thought! Likewise with positive thought.

Thought is extremely powerful and is at the core of creation. Because thought is energy and as energy knows no bounds, it continues to travel to the far ends of the universe. The outstanding benefit to this universal truth is that those healers who choose can heal a person anywhere in the world without actually being physically present. A healer can direct the healing energy to the patient by thought. The disadvantage means that if you have a negative thought about anyone, that person will receive negative energy, especially if it is sent in anger or some other highly emotional state. It does not matter where they are located!

It is believed by many that whatever is sent out returns to the source. This is true and is part of Karma, the law of cause and effect, but there is more to it than that. As energy attracts like energy, anger being negative energy will return as anger, or even in some other negative form, having gathered to it like energies. This can be devastating.

We have to learn not to send our anger to anyone, even in thought. We must learn to control our emotions as the power emotional outbursts generate is damaging to all in the energetic vicinity. I am not suggesting that emotions are to be ignored or suppressed, but we must learn how to respond to situations in a way that is not harmful.

Positive thoughts and confident, happy moods receive the universal energy in the same way, so why would we want to be anything else other than happy? It is a choice each individual has to make, and for some, ongoing through the day.

Mental telepathy is one of the functions of the mind that we need to be more proficient in. People that are either more aware or sensitive, or have a very strong attachment to someone by bonding or love, actually receive mental messages when someone thinks of them. With a little practice we can learn to recognize this and enhance the gift so that one is more in control rather than just randomly sending and receiving.

It is not necessary to be psychically developed to experience mental telepathy, it is automatic when passion accompanies the thought. For example, a person in fear in a desperate situation gives an internal cry for help and the person "called" receives the energy vibration, knows something is wrong, and instinctively with whom. Distance does not matter.

Another example is when someone dies and their presence is felt at the side of a loved one at the moment before transition, or what we call death. The spirit leaving the body has come to say good-bye. These are natural occurrences caused by thought. When the spirit is disconnected from its body, the mind remains the same as it was before leaving the body. This allows the spirit the freedom to wander wherever the mind takes it in an instant.

When we become aware that a spirit is present, we do not have time to think. This causes us to disregard our belief systems. Even those who believe that spirit exists very often block communication with the expectation of *how* spirit will communicate. In truth there are many different ways spirit communicates. Thought is so very powerful. How many times have you thought of someone, the phone rings and there they are?

Who contacted who? Were they already dialing when they popped into your mind, or did your thought cause them to dial your number?

It is not only the conscious thought that works its magic. When we sleep our thoughts do not stop, we are just not conscious of them. All unconscious thoughts also reach their destination, whether positive or negative. Therefore whether your mind is in turmoil or not it is advisable to clear it before you retire by any method you feel is right for you. Certainly meditation or conscious breathing are two ways, or maybe listening to some relaxing music is your way. There are many ways, and I am sure you can find yours. Go to sleep happy!

CREATIVE THOUGHT

As has been mentioned, energy attracts like energy. Therefore it stands to reason that if we can learn to apply correct thought to our everyday lives we can eventually heal ourselves, attracting the necessary situations for our spiritual growth. By right thought, we can prevent attracting further unnecessary illness or negative situations to occur; for they will only continue to occur until we have learned this lesson. We all take our time to learn this lesson, and during the period of learning our energy is also teaching others. Do not be hard on yourself. You do not realize all that is going on or why.

As we are on a journey of discovery and learning, we are bound to make mistakes and these mistakes slow us up. Because of this, and a lack of patience, some people judge themselves too harshly. This creates new situations and feelings. We have to make choices, and if we were clever enough to make all the right choices, I really don't think we would need to be here. No one is so evolved that he or she does not have any more evolving to do, and if we are to evolve, then we need to experience new things.

One question that I have been frequently asked is the effect of our choices and behavior on others. When we realize that by our choice, we have caused pain either to ourselves, or to someone else, we face the lesson of letting go of the feeling of guilt. Yes, let go! Remember we are not only in situations for our benefit, but at the same time we are acting a part to provide others with an experience also. I must point out that it does not give anyone license to consciously create pain for another, or to put aside feelings of compassion.

The secret of a smoother journey is to allow experiences into your life and allow others their experiences. Rather than creating them, let life flow. Your soul is in charge, trust it. Give up manipulating your self and others by actions or innuendo. It takes careful watching of the words we speak and also our powerful thoughts.

I have mentioned right thought, but what is right thought? We are all on our unique paths and it is different for each one, but there is a common bond and way for us all. That way is the need to give and receive love. Let go of all that is standing in the way of love. Let go of the feelings of fear, blame, resentment and guilt for they are some of the barriers. Use your thought to create different feelings. Realize that everyone is here to learn, that the only difference is that we are all at different stages of our learning and experiencing in different ways, and remember we are all here to play a part for each other.

The mind is hard to control but there is one body that is far harder!

THE EMOTIONAL BODY

It is the emotional body that is the hardest to control therefore the hardest to deal with. We have to learn here to allow our pain, but not to hold on to it. To feel our grief, but to move through it. Once we realize that we can alter how we feel by changing our thoughts, the emotions are a lot easier to deal with.

Each time we experience a situation or relationship that causes us emotional pain, there is an indication that it is something for us to learn and evolve from. The attitudes we acquire play a role in determining how quickly we evolve as we move through the emotional states that these situations create.

The following are the three situations that promote the quickest growth for us!

1. The passing of someone close to us.
2. Divorce.
3. Moving house.

Our true aim is to accept what is, with love and not resentment, guilt, or a sense of abandonment. We have to come to the realization that we are not "victims", instead we are all serving one another, "acting" the part that will show us where we are through our "reactions". In other words we are all mirrors for one another, therefore there is no need for forgiveness. No one has done anything that isn't necessary at that time. But then, contradicting myself, until we truly understand this, there is a real need for forgiveness.

Most of us have experienced a situation where we lost control of our emotions. Maybe we reacted with an uncontrollable fit of weeping. Crying is a wonderful release but prolonged can cause self-pity. Depending on the control we have over our thoughts and the ability to change them, we can grow or get stuck in pity. Pity, whether for ourselves or for others, is a negative energy for it takes us deeper into the victim role. What is needed here is understanding of the situation along with love and support. Empathy and compassion are positive energies and therefore supportive of the person's growth.

Grief is felt several times in an incarnation. It is a natural reaction to loss and occurs when we lose someone close to us either in death or separation; we also go through a period of grief when we lose a pet. I have noticed during my time healing and teaching that there is a grief that is felt when we move on from our old self in growth.

The purpose of each incarnation is spiritual growth so we go through several stages in each. We experience a lesson, we learn that lesson and in the learning our energy changes. We have then moved on and as our energy has changed so old energies are no longer compatible with us and fall away. Most of us experience that the mind has not kept up with the change though and very often confusion and grief follow. One man told me it was like loosing his best friend for he didn't know his new self yet. He was fortunate in having someone explain the path to him and he moved through quickly to become a freer and happier person. Just recently I had a call from another man who has been studying with me who stated, "I don't know who I am, but I'm not who I have ever been." For myself I can look back to the original me and see the different stages I went through to reach who I am today. I can see when I stopped struggling and trying to swim upstream, just by how my life started to flow and I started to feel so good. For years I had felt so bad! I can also see when I came into my own power and stopped following the choices of others.

Disciplining the emotional body is not easy; Oh, but it is so rewarding!

GETTING HELP

Sometimes we find that we need outside help when we are at the point of releasing old emotional pain. There are many different healing disciplines. Always choose one with which you feel comfortable.

Energy Healing – As everything is energy, it follows that all forms of healing operate at an energetic level. This includes Eastern medicine, Western medicine and the metaphysical approaches.

Following are some of the many therapies readily available, where the specific intent of the therapist is to work with the energy of the client. The intent of the therapist creates the method the body receives, each method working in a specific way and creating different results. As mentioned before, always choose a method and a therapist with which you feel comfortable.

Some forms of natural energy healing—

Soul Path Healing – Tuning into and working through the soul of the client that in my experience is the only intelligence that knows what is required for the healing and growth of that individual.

Psychic Healing – in this method the clients and/or the healer's Spirit Guides are involved in guiding the healing energy.

Sound – sound through it's vibratory rate can be either destroyer or healer and with the right facilitator is a very powerful method of transmuting energies.

Spiritual Counseling – understanding that there is purpose and why going through different situations changes our attitudes, and in turn helps lessens the pain.

Rebirthing – a method using different breaths, allowing some to experience their physical birth and releasing the trauma attached to the unconscious memory of that event and others.

Psycho Therapy – a method to mentally explore the psychological reactions to situations and learning to deal with the cause.

Note – preferably followed by Healing.

A few more of the methods that promote Healing are—

Aromatherapy

Chiropractic

Crystal Healing

Cranial Sacral

Light Touch

Magnetic healing

Massage

Network Chiropractic

Past Life regression

Polarity Healing
Reflexology
Reiki

Again I say, when receiving a therapy, you need to feel safe and comfortable with the therapist. Also before leaving at the end of the session make sure you feel complete and secure. If you do not, speak up!

If you still feel that the therapist has left you vulnerable, close your aura. This is done simply with a thought of closure, or you can imagine wrapping your energy round your body like wings.

Of course no one must expect to be totally healed in one session, especially if the condition has been with the person for a long time, but I have experienced channeling a total healing on more than one occasion.

I do not know the reason why one person is totally healed and another is not, for as a "channel" of healing it is neither any of my business, nor my responsibility, to determine what is correct for the client. That issue lies between the client and a Power higher than mine. My realization of the experience is that when a person reaches a certain point on the soul's path, they are ready to release the old and go on to the new. This happens over and over again for the energy of an experience is felt and held at several different levels. The levels can only be released individually as the person becomes ready. This explains why some people think that they have dealt with and completed with the reactions to a past experience, only to have it surface again and again.

When a person is ready, I believe that it would not matter whether they had come to me or to some other healer channeling God's energy. The healing would have still occurred. Being a teacher as well as a healer, I know that I have been guided to prepare many for their transitions both to continue in the present incarnation and for leaving it. I feel so privileged to have been chosen to help so many souls on their path.

PRAYER AS A HEALER

"For everyone who asks, receives". Matthew. 7:8

Prayer is underestimated as a healer. Talk to God, to your master, to your guides, and don't forget the angels. Talk as you would to any friend that you love and respect. Say what is in your heart. Not one prayer is left unheard or unanswered. The difference between the talking to unseen energies and your friends is that it is not necessary to say anything out loud. You can pray quietly in your mind and receive complete understanding. Maybe this is the best therapy of all, as you can say all the things that are on your mind and in your heart. Share all those memories and feelings that you have kept locked inside – those things that you have not told anyone because you believed you would not be understood and therefore would be judged. You will be surprised at the joy you feel when the burden is lifted by just sharing your secrets with a nonjudgmental deity.

LETTING GO

To one who has been holding on to everything all their lives, this seems an impossible task. Not so! Once you have done it a couple of times it gets easier. There is not really any magic formula except you have to sincerely intend to let go. A lot of people have an underlying fear that the void will not be filled.

The first thing to let go of is fear. Love can replace fear. The next step is to work on any old emotional memories. These can cause some to hold grudges or resentments. We also have to let go of the attachment to people and possessions. A lot of letting go!

As with all energy work, it is the underlying belief that determines the outcome of the procedure, so be honest with yourself and allow your true feelings and beliefs to come into your consciousness. Do you really want to let go or are you just kidding yourself?

On the following pages are two methods, in the way I perform them, to help you to release your old self and help you to start to live in your own Truth. These rituals have been proven powerful by the students and clients who have used them. For you who feel that some one has done you wrong, the Forgiveness formula is extremely effective. If you wish to strengthen it even more follow it with Cutting the link. If you have physically broken a relationship yet you still feel psychically connected, try Cutting the link.

There are also books on forgiveness and cutting links. "The Only Diet There Is" by Sondra Ray published by Celestial Arts, Berkley CA. USA deals with forgiveness, and "Cutting The Ties" by Phyllis Krystal published by Aura Book. LA. USA deals with the links.

I recommend these for those of you who wish to explore and understand more on the subjects.

FORGIVENESS FORMULA

This is a very powerful way to change the effect one person has on another through their psychic link, whether they are alive or have passed on. This does not mean that the one forgiven will physically disappear from your life, but rather that the relationship will be on a different level from the time of the successful completion of the process.

You must strictly follow the instructions, as this method is a magic formula. Unless you complete each session each day for the full seven days with no gaps, you will find yourself repeating the diet all over again.

Commit yourself to your healing. Get yourself a legal pad and make sure you are in a place where you will not be disturbed.

PREPARATION

Shutting your eyes, center your energies by taking a few slow, regular breaths and allow the breath to go deeper into your lungs than you normally do. Ask within yourself for your masters and your guides to help you with your forgiveness, then begin your writing.

METHOD

Seventy times for seven days write down these exact words. After completing the sentence, close your eyes and feel the response. Now write the response down exactly as it came into your mind. When this is done, center your energy and repeat the procedure.

I (your name) **FORGIVE YOU** (name of whomever you are forgiving) **COMPLETELY.** For instance, if I were forgiving my mother I would write:

"I, MARGARITE, FORGIVE YOU, MOM, COMPLETELY."

but if I was forgiving a previous husband who called me Maggy, I would write:

"I, MAGGY, FORGIVE YOU, DON, COMPLETELY."

You need to use the names you are both familiar with in any relationship you are dealing with. If my mother had called me by a nickname, I would have used that. As stated above, after writing each line close your eyes for a moment to allow the response to rise from your subconscious mind into your conscious mind. Immediately write it down exactly, whatever it is, even if it is *"There is nothing to forgive"*. Some feel the response rising so quickly that they do not need to close their eyes. Some do not feel a response at all; in fact they see no need to do the forgiveness at all. They believe that they have completed the forgiveness previously. I have found that there are still things that have to be addressed. I am not saying that this is always the case, but very often – in fact nine times out of ten – it is. Persevere and you will release both yourself and the one you are forgiving from the chains created by blame and shame.

Forgive only one person a week, as you will need all of your inner powers to deal with the process. We sometimes remember what it is in this life that causes us to need to forgive, but we seldom remember the other existences that brought us to the situations in this life. This is why we say "completely".

As soon as you have completed this exercise, destroy the sheet you have written by any of the four elements – FIRE, WATER, EARTH or AIR – or any combination of them.

DO NOT KEEP IT!

Margarite Westo

CUTTING THE LINKS

As we live our lives a psychic link is created with each person with whom we have had contact, even if it is only a casual acquaintance. The link is a line of energy from one soul to another; you could liken it to a fine silk thread. If our acquaintance grows into a deeper relationship, whether through love or any other emotion, the link becomes stronger, and the silk thread appears to grow into a thick cord. This happens with anyone you deal with regularly, even if your only link with them is on the phone. If one is in a relationship and becomes possessive, then the cord can turn into a chain or maybe even shackles. This link is not a physical thing and is not automatically broken when we either break the relationship or they pass on. We are discussing energy here, so there are no barriers to cutting the link other than the barriers we create with our mind. It matters not where the other soul is located, whether or not we are physically in touch with them; one can release oneself and at the same time release the other soul. When we realize that we carry with us, in the form of energy, whatever we have not dealt with before we die, it is only common sense to try to deal with whatever we can while we are still living.

PREPARATION

Shut your eyes, center your energies by taking a few slow, regular breaths, and allow the breath to go deeper into your lungs than you normally do.

METHOD

Sit or lie down in the position you find most relaxing, then take yourself to the alpha state by continuing with the breathing described above. Once you are at this depth of consciousness, create a picture in your mind of the figure eight drawn on the ground large enough to take two chairs placed one in each end of the figure, facing each other,(see diagram 1). You will place yourself in one chair placing the person you wish to cut the link with in the other. If you have something you wish to say, now is the time to say it. Do not hold back. Express how you feel – maybe how they hurt you – or tell them how much you love them. If you need to forgive them, do so, and if you need them to forgive you, ask them to forgive you. Whatever it is, get it said. There will not be a more suitable time.

When you have finished, with your mind's eye, look down your body to see if any strings are attached to you anywhere from your head down to your toes. When you find one, look along it to see where it is attached to the other person. Once you have found the two ends, you find that there is the biggest pair of shears you have ever seen lying by your side. You struggle to pick them up, as they are just about as big as you are. You cut the link as close to your body as you can, then you cut the link as close to the other body as you can.

Now it is time to destroy the cord, or whatever else you have found, by one of the four purifying elements of this planet – earth, air, fire or water. Which one to use will come into your mind, but here are a few suggestions from people who have used this procedure.

CUTTING THE LINKS

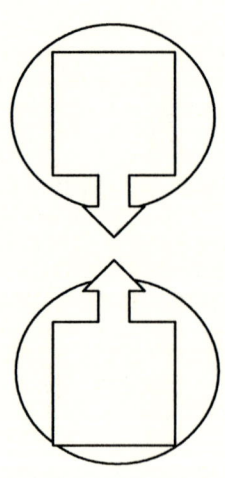 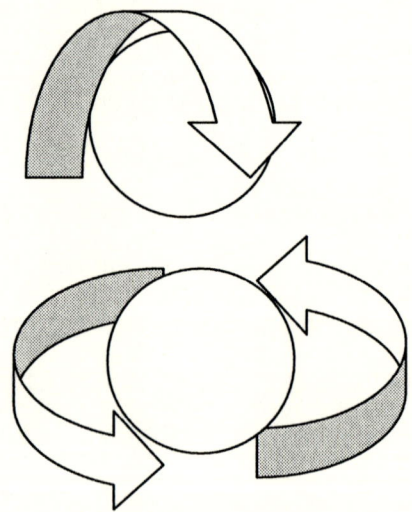

Place two chairs facing as shown above

Diagram 1

send light around the eight following the arrows.

Diagram 2

FIRE You could create a big furnace, open the door, and toss the cord in. It will immediately be consumed by the fire and change into purified energy.

WATER You could put it in the deepest part of the ocean for water purification.

AIR You could call up a hurricane or tornado for air purification.

EARTH You could bury it deep under a mountain or in a spot that is sacred to you for earth purification.

Whichever way you feel at the time will be the right way for you. Be creative!

When you have completed that stage, it is time to start working with the light to heal and protect you both. Sending light around the figure eight, allowing it to run as long as you feel it is necessary.

For those that have found it difficult to visualize light, I suggested a little train running on the track of the figure eight that train being made of light (see diagram 2). This will not only build up a wall between you but also around you.

Stay quiet for a while, then look down your body again. There may be more than one link to the same person. If you find another, repeat the procedure until you feel all is clear.

You may feel emotional for a while afterwards! Do not attempt to do more than one person in the same day unless the process happens naturally or you feel very clear about it.

Margarite Westo

You need to cut the links with everyone in your life, past and present, including relatives and friends. This will not cause the person to go away physically: instead it will change the relationship in a very healthy way. Start by cutting the links to the first one who comes into your mind. This procedure frees us to move on with our spiritual growth!

THE SPIRITUAL BODY

Now we come to the spiritual "body". This is the one that is the most misunderstood and/or mistreated by many of us. There are still people with the belief that we do not become spirit until we die. The fact is, we are spirit living in a body, spirit incarnate. This spirit neither is born nor dies. It is the part of us that knows why we are here, why we chose our particular parents, our particular skin color, the particular country, and the religious or non-religious environment surrounding us as we grow. Yes, we chose all of these things, and also the time we were born.

The purpose for incarnating is to learn and evolve, each one of us coming from a unique background to learn our lessons in our own unique way. Sometimes it seems that we have to repeat our lessons over and over again before we understand. There are several depths of understanding to achieve before we accept it and make it part of our own Truth.

By Truth, I do not mean the absence of a lie. When you live in your own Truth you live your life, make your decisions, and treat others from your own point of evolvement. You no longer live according to what you think others expect of you, or because you are concerned with what others will think of you if you do not conform to the general consensus. When you go against your own truth your physical body will react, and this in turn will lower your energy vibration working on your emotional body leading to a feeling of guilt or confusion the result of which is in a mood swing. Take note and change your energies to bring in a higher vibration. This uplifts the spirit and you can be out of the down swing very quickly indeed.

THE HEALING EXERCISE

The way to change your energies is simple and enjoyable. The most important thing to remember is that you will achieve whatever intentions you have in mind; therefore you must be absolutely clear and strong in your focus.

This is the exercise.

Sit or lay in a comfortable position. Keeping your mouth shut tightly, lips together, draw or suck breath in through your nose from your throat by tightening the muscles at the back of the tongue. These are the ones you use when you swallow. Try it. Swallow but be aware of what is happening in your throat. If you stop the swallow halfway you will find that you cannot breathe. Now partly relax the tongue muscles allowing yourself to draw in a small amount of air at the same time. You could feel the air going into your throat. It is these muscles at the back of the tongue that you use to regulate how much air you breathe in at a time. If you feel your nostrils move you are not doing it correctly; you are pulling the breath through your nose as you do when you breathe normally. When this occurs do not give up, try it again. It is well worth it. When you do it correctly you will hear your breath inside your head, rather like the sound of the ebbing and flowing of the tide. It is good to practice this breath daily until it

becomes second nature to you. When you have mastered this you have the basic breath for self-healing, and having mastered it, now is the time to put your intention with it.

These are some of the things that I know have been relieved with intention and this breathing method.

Release of stress, easing pain, lowering blood pressure, insomnia, release of old energies drawing in new energies, help through an emotional time, clearing thoughts when making a decision, feeding creativity, writer's block, and much more!

I must emphasize that your intention determines where your energy goes, hence the importance of the clarity of your intention.

The breath should be as slow as you possibly can make it but still be comfortable. You should not feel any stress from the breathing. Keep the out breath exactly the same length as the in breath. You do not hold the breath at either the top or the bottom; the aim is a completely round breath. This becomes easier with practice. The effort you put in will determine the amount of benefit you receive.

The greatest long-term benefit is the capability of linking with your spirit, your higher self or your soul, that part of you that knows what is right for you at any given moment.

If you practice this method, after a period of time you will experience a change in your thought patterns and therefore in the way you approach everything you do. You will also find you make decisions more from feelings than logic. All this will be because you are in tune with your soul and allowing it to guide you. This is something that will develop naturally as long as you practice your focused breathing with that intention. When you reach this point you will generally experience your bodies as one. The next step is to attain oneness with the universe.

Keeping compatible company is so important, I have to mention it again. Because energy is magnetic, it continuously draws to it energies from all around as we move through the day. The person we are with could be the sweetest person we know, but if that person has been mixing with the sick, maybe working with addicts or the homeless, or maybe spending time with a negative person, then the negative energy could be unconsciously picked up and carried until some other person unconsciously magnetizes it away. Unless you are aware and your energies are centered, this could be you. It is not only people that carry energy. We can go into a restaurant that is empty of people and still pick up on the positive and negativity energy. Everything absorbs energy. This is why some places we visit make us feel that we cannot wait to leave, whilst others make us feel good and we want to prolong our visit.

The earth also holds energy. Even though the ground is tilled or buildings erected, the ground holds the energy of past events. A battlefield is a good example. An experienced psychic can alter this energy. The method would be to communicate with any spirits that have attached themselves to the area, releasing the memory and bringing in Light.

Once we have reached the point of tuning in to our higher self, the knowing of what is correct for us will be automatic and so instantaneous that in time we will know whether or not to accept certain invitations or meet with certain people even as we are being asked.

Follow your feelings, for this is the only way to gain trust in yourself. With each positive experience, you will open more and more to the knowledge within you, and this is immense, for within the cells of your body you carry the memory of all that has been and all that will be. It is more widely understood now that each one brings other life memories into this incarnation. Along with these memories come historical, religious, racial, and planetary memories. All of these unconscious memories underlie our attitudes and decisions. This is why to become familiar with connecting to your inner self is of the utmost importance.

One way to protect yourself from negative energies is to imagine yourself in a bubble of white light while gently performing the breathing. For this you breathe with your eyes open, with the intention of staying in positive and loving energy. This way the negative energy cannot reach you, for you are focused and therefore your energy is centered.

Although we need to take responsibility for our own healing and life, that does not mean we cannot receive help from others when we need it. In fact one of our lessons may be to learn to ask for help, then to learn to receive it without thinking that we have failed ourselves.

This is not meaning that we hand over the responsibility, we can accept help but still keep control. Having realized that we need help, the next step is to find a therapist that we feel comfortable with. Then when we are with the therapist we need to participate in our own healing by being open and receptive. Staying aware enables us to know whether this is the right thing for us, not just another false lead put out by others to teach us a different lesson. It pays to stay in awareness! If it feels right, then allow what needs to be, whatever that happens to be at the time, however strange it seems to your mind.

Self-healing in the end means being in your own Power, living in your own Truth, taking responsibility, and caring for your mind, your emotions, your body, and your spirit. Healing means becoming whole.

Once there, at first the joy will be overwhelming, and you will want everyone around you to feel that joy. Spread the word and support them in their efforts, but if they do not want to follow your lead that is their choice. You have sown the seed, and it will stay in the dark until it is the right time for it to germinate. When the person is ready and capable to handle whatever the process of growth brings into their life, their life will start to change and their journey will become one of awareness.

Do not be concerned with what others are doing, for you cannot change anything outside yourself. You can change only yourself. In changing yourself you will find your energy field is causing things and people around to change slowly. All you have to do is be yourself.

Do not hold on to the past, or you will block the flow of energy in the present. Now is the only time that is real. The past is gone and the future is not here yet, so the energy you put into holding on to the past is lost in illusion, as is the energy you put into your dreams for the future. Allow yourself to live now, to be yourself. You cannot move on to anything other than what you are now without fully accepting what you are. Once you accept yourself as you are now, then you have a basis for improvement. You cannot change the past but you can release it. And the future? What you do now determines the future.

Ask your higher self for guidance and help, then accept whatever comes as necessary for your growth, and above all, give thanks. The things you used to see as big problems will not seem so bad, and you will be able to move through them. When those uninvited thoughts of doubt come in, accept them, then immediately let them go.

RELEASE, RELEASE, CONTINUALLY RELEASE. NO GUILT. NO RESENTMENT. NO BLAME. NO SICKNESS!!!

INTRODUCTION TO THE SESSIONS

In the past, when I had the initial soul path healing session with a new client, I was guided to read the soul energy before they received hands on healing. As I was reading the energy, I received pictures that were related to the cause of the challenge they had brought to be healed. During the reading the energy was brought to the surface to be transmuted. To enable the energy to be read the client needed to be quiet and centered. Back then in the nineteen eighties, I found that of the majority that were inclined to come for soul path healing many already knew how to center their energy through meditation.

I always have believed that we can do what we need to do, as everything is perfect and works in its own time. It was when I was at the Berry Hill center that I received and was prompted to use the 'balloon method' for centering for all that came. On experiencing this method it was obvious that meditation for soul path readings was not enough; I was delighted with the clarity and speed at which I could see and deal with the causes with this new method.

The call came from Jack. He had bumped into an old friend that he hadn't seen for some time. Realizing the change in Jack's mental state, his friend suggested that he call me to see if healing would help. He felt that it would. Jack was the President of a large corporation and had considerable knowledge of business and physical sports, but no knowledge of anything metaphysical or of natural mental relaxation. After some thought and adjustment to his attitude towards the intangible, and because he had tried all other avenues of assistance, he called and made an appointment. Jack lived in the east of England and I was situated in the West Country. It was with some considerable organizing of his time and much physical effort that he managed to keep his appointments. Previously he had been using the western method of drug therapy under a doctor's supervision to relax and get over his enormous stress and depression. Naturally I would not tell him to stop his medication or even to cut down, but his doctor did as his healing proceeded. It was during Jack's first visit that I received the instructions for the balloon method of centering.

Before a client arrived I would prepare myself and my healing space by meditation etc. and would place two chairs facing each other about 2 to 3 feet apart. When the clients arrived I did not chat, but seated them immediately asking that they take a few deep breaths. This helped me to stay in the consciousness I had attained when preparing for the session.

Jack was a bit of a challenge. He wanted to treat the session as though he was at the doctor's office, understandable, as this was all he knew. At that first session he even found it difficult to remove his jacket and loose his tie, and I had to insist. He also removed his shoes at my request. To help him to feel more comfortable I let him talk. I stayed centered and quiet as he rambled on about many things including all that was wrong with him while I quietly asked for help from his guides. At last I found myself telling him that he had told me enough. I explained to him that I wanted him to bring all his energies into his heart area. He said he didn't know how to, and that is when my energy changed and I channeled the Balloon Method.

I was surprised at the clarity of what I was seeing. I could pretty well tell the dates of the incarnations that I was viewing from the style of dress. It was more difficult to say where these scenes were taking place. As I related what I had experienced I realized that healing had been achieved for many of the other incomplete life situations. We finished with a hand's on healing and by the time the session was over my new client was asking to book the next session.

From then on I used this method of centering and have taught it in my classes to those who have decided to use the soul path method of healing. In the following chapters I have related a few of the many interesting sessions that I have experienced. I have included the instructions at the end of this book for those of you that would like to practice helping others to bring their energies in to their center point.

Margarite Westo

LEARN TO FLY

I was away from Sylvan and using a friend's living room to see the people who had requested healing sessions. She used it for her own method of healing and had decided it would be good to replace the original open fire with a gas fire, a more efficient and a much cleaner way of heating.

My client arrived and as we centered ourselves before the session, I could already feel the heaviness surrounding her. I tuned in and immediately saw her caught up in many different beliefs, which were appearing to me as wings held tight to her and made of something as heavy as lead. Each feather was a different concept she had either heard, or created, but had not let go of. I realized that her being tied up so tightly in beliefs had been going on for lifetimes. I opened my mouth to tell her how I could hear her soul screaming for freedom, but before I could say a word there was a loud thud behind the gas fire. It was accompanied by an equally loud screech of terror.

It is common for birds to nest in chimneys in England so the usual procedure is to place a wire guard over the top of the stack. It was obvious that the workmen had not done this when they had installed the fire. I knew that one of the young birds had grown too heavy causing the nest to collapse, and the unfortunate chick to fall into the fireplace. In an open fireplace the bird would be picked up and nursed until it could be taken back outside, but in an enclosed fireplace like this one, there was no way to reach the unfortunate bird due to the gas fixtures.

My client had a hysterical reaction to this occurrence, definitely an over reaction. I instinctively knew that the universe was providing the trapped chick that could not fly as a reflection of my client's dilemma. The chick would sacrifice itself and die in its trap to enable my client's underlying feelings to surface, ready for the healing to take place.

I told her my understanding of the situation and she broke down weeping uncontrollably. She told me she was always attracted to people that had new ideas, so these were the friends and relationships she chose. She would buy into their ideas completely but would immediately go on when she found someone with a new idea, which would not take too long. She would then take on board the new concept and the new relationship without completing with the now out dated one.

I tuned into her and found that her soul was indeed crying out for help. This had been her pattern, going back to a lifetime when her soul, incarnated as a male, had chosen incorrectly. As his choice had led to the death of hundreds of people who relied on him for their safety, he at that time swore never to be in that situation again. Consequently, she had brought the energy of his decision with her into this incarnation. This underlying energy made her fearful of making her own decisions for fear of being wrong and causing others pain. She then feared making the decision to let go for the same reason. Here was a catch 22 situation. The old energy needed to be transmuted and then released.

This was one of the early cases that taught me so much about how we are in control of our own destiny. What we do, what we say, the belief system that we have acquired, influence what we will experience in the future. We will unconsciously choose situations that will cause the original energies to rise in us to be dealt with. We respond to these situations with instinctive reactions that we cannot explain. Until we have our energies cleared we are not in our own power. After we have taken back our power, we may choose situations that will test us to determine if, now that we have learned to be in our own power, we will mishandle the power and use it to profit at the expense of others.

All I could do for my client was to suggest that she let the healing energies work for her. In this case the inclination to move from one belief to the next worked for her.

The next time I was in the area she came for a second session. I could see that she was much lighter and freer than she was at the first visit. I have not seen her since, but heard that she was in a stable relationship and had a steady job, both good signs, as she had neither before her healing.

DELIA'S MAGIC MAN

This time Delia herself rang me up to ask for Healing. Delia was 8 years old, her brother John was 6, and her baby brother Andy was just 5 1/2 months. They lived on the coast in Cornwall, a county in the West Country of England. The cottage was two minutes from the beach, the ideal place for them to grow up. The two older children attended the local school so they had lots of companions to share the joy of their area with. They had moved from the City of Bristol and now that they had settled down they both enjoyed their lives in the village by the sea.

Both of their parents had received Healing from me when they felt it was time to accept some help with their growth, were feeling off color, or needed a boost in energy. They knew through their own experience that healing brought out suppressed memories or feelings that they needed to let go of, but when Delia called me, neither they nor I were prepared for what was to transpire.

The children had also had Healing on and off since they were very young and they loved it, always feeling happy and healthy the next morning. I must add that the majority of the time I did transfer healing for them. This took place when they had gone to bed with one parent present.

As I said, Delia called me herself to ask for Healing not only for herself, but for her brothers as well. After I had agreed, her mother came to the phone to arrange the time and to tell me how they all were. That evening the sessions went as usual as far as I was concerned, so I closed the session, at the same time protecting them and thought that was the end of it.

The next day was a really busy day for me. I didn't give the family in Cornwall any thought as I arranged a trip to the other side of England to visit a handicapped baby. I was taken by surprise when I got a call from the mother to tell me that all the children had been awful all day, and Delia had not even attended school.

Delia had got up that morning and had come down stairs wearing a brown paper bag on her head. Mum didn't take much notice, as she thought she was having a bit of fun. What did catch mum's notice was the fact that she had buttoned herself up incorrectly, as she was normally a very particular child. Delia continued to wear the bag as they headed for school. Now mum was getting a bit suspicious! While driving to school, she questioned Delia and got nothing from her except that Delia did not want to go to school. Now mum knew that there was something really wrong. Delia was not a child to stay away from school. The teachers were also concerned. After checking around the school to make sure that nothing had happened to put Delia off wanting to attend, mum took Delia home again. During the course of the day Delia spoke a lot about magic, but this did not seem odd for a child. It was decided that I would repeat the healing that evening.

Again I settled down to do a Transfer Healing first on Delia, then on John and then on baby Andy. I tuned into Delia and all went without incident until just before the end when I became aware of an excruciating pain in my left leg which quickly moved down to my left foot and out through my toes leaving me quite clear. At the same time I saw a little elf like man wearing a bright hat and waistcoat. He was about the same height as Delia and had an old wrinkled face.

He was pleasant enough, but I knew immediately that this was what had been wrong with Delia. Inspiration told me that she had created this very real figure out of a fictional character she had encountered in a story. This may have been when she was a lot younger, at an age when presumably innocent stories can influence a child's mind. It is at this time that the belief that the character is real can cause a sensitive child to give life to a fictional character, whether created by their imagination, or by someone else's.

I called back the day after the second Healing. Dad answered the phone and I told him what I had experienced. He told me she had been reading a lot of Enid Blyton and we assumed between us that it would be one of these characters. It brought back memories of my own childhood and the elves in her books.

Her mum came on the phone and I repeated the conversation again. Then mum came up with a more likely elf! Mum suddenly remembered that Delia had continually spoken of magic since the first Healing, and recognizing the wrinkled face I saw she came up with an old elf who was a do-gooder; a nice friendly elf who helped whoever he could by performing magic. Mum and Delia had read several stories about his deeds when she had been younger. As Delia was a child who liked to help people, we realized that she wished she was able to perform magic like this do-gooder elf. We knew that we had hit on the right storybook character.

To those who have never realized the power of thought it seems impossible that we can create a creature to grow along with us. Whether you believe this is possible or not, it would be prudent for you to be aware of your child's, and your own, mental intake, for a creation of the mind can be friend or foe. I, personally, am well aware of that power. During sessions in my healing room I have come across some incredible creatures that have been creating havoc in clients lives. Fortunately I have been able to deal with them in the majority of cases. I have not managed to eliminate the ones that the *owners* have not wanted to part with.

Another example of the fact that if we can get to the cause of our situation, our attitudes or illnesses, whether on our own or with help, we can change, by releasing the old and becoming healthy.

Delia is today a loving, healthy, vibrant woman, highly intelligent, and probably doesn't even remember her MAGIC MAN.

LINGERING DEATH

It wasn't until the second appointment that I saw how deeply Nancy had suppressed her memories.

In amongst her balloons I saw a group of colorless ones, not even white, but absolutely colorless. This was the first time I had come across an absolutely colorless one. Instinct told me that this was a memory that was too painful for the client to face on her own. Her soul had waited, not only for the correct time to allow it to surface, but also for the time when she would have help in releasing it once it had.

She had come to me originally because she had been diagnosed with lupus and she also had cancer. The first time she came we did not get to the cause of the disease, so I was pleased to see that her soul felt that she was now ready to deal with whatever came up.

The area looked something like I would imagine Pompei would have looked, I felt it was around the time of the Trojan wars. I knew that we were on a Greek island, but which one I could not tell. She was a young woman dressed in a white toga with flowers in her hair. She was sitting on a marble bench that seemed to be on a patio attached to the house. The house had marble pillars yet was only a one-story structure. Her attention was on a big, brutish looking man who was obviously of high rank. He stood a few feet away with his back to her. I was aware that she felt anxious and hopeless as she watched him looking off into the distance. I knew at once that she was a slave and he was her master yet he treated her as his wife. As I watched, a girl I knew to be their daughter came onto the patio. She was about six years old, dressed in a similar manner to her mother. At the same time a boy of about three years old peeped around one of the pillars at the end of the structure.

The story started to unravel in my mind. He had been one of the top army generals and was also related to the ruling family of his particular country of birth. The present ruler had exiled him and his household to this island since the general was not in agreement with how the country was being ruled. The general was very popular with the masses, and the ruler was frightened that he would be aided by them to return and take over the country. He was so afraid in fact, that he had placed in the exiled household one whose job it was to add poison to their food that would work very slowly. He had decided on slow poison, for if it were obvious that they were poisoned he would be immediately suspected and the people would rise up against him anyway. Therefore he had devised this plan that would make it look as though they had some disease that slowly drained away their life's energy, a debilitating disease. Like Lupus!

Nancy watched as her children and her master slowly got closer to death and went through what all mothers go through when they see their children suffering and cannot do anything about it. She just watched them wasting away and found that this was a greater pain than her own physical pain. She blamed her master for the pain their children were experiencing, and a hate grew in her which she had not overcome when she finally died.

I realized that the cause of the cancer had not yet surfaced; and decided I had better go back inside her consciousness and have another look. In another lifetime I saw the same soul of the brutish man having the same type of personality, but this time was playing the role of the father. Her soul, this time, had chosen the role of the sensitive son, who loved music and the arts, and having no stomach for drinking and womanizing, or for war.

They were German and it was at the time of the Great War, or the First World War as it has come to be known. He was about seventeen or eighteen and his father was not pleased to have a sensitive son. He felt it reflected on him. It made him feel less of a man to have been involved in the creation of such a sissy. He wanted a boy who was very macho, like himself. He thought he was doing the right thing enrolling his son in the navy as this would 'make a man of him'.

After training the boy was assigned to a U-Boat, and this is where he suffered his greatest abuse. As he was sensitive, he was taken to be effeminate and the crew raped and beat him repeatedly, in spite of his protests. The captain of the boat knew what was going on, but as it did not interfere with the running of the boat he looked the other way. He came through his life experience with hate for his father and resentment for pretty well everyone else. It seemed that nobody understood him. He died in the U-Boat and carried that hate and resentment with him, in energy form, through into his death.

The soul brought that energy into this life where it had been brewing and creating situations to help her to release it. It had been buried so deep that, although the client had been through a lot of therapy, she had never been able to reach this point before.

The soul that has been the master and the father in previous lives was also with her in this life. Nancy needed to understand that we are all playing roles to serve each other. She had to come to the realization that there is no reason for hate, and overcome it. She had to learn to let go of the energy of resentment so that she could allow her relationships to change in this lifetime, and her body required the opportunity to become healthy again.

When clients feel that they need a break from healing sessions, or when I feel that they need a break, I keep them on the prayer list until I feel their needs to have been met. This I did with this lady.

OFF THE PATH!

Expensively and tastefully dressed, he sat opposite me and I wondered what he needed from me. Richard seemed to be successful and the energy about him told me that he was well balanced and self-confident.

I tuned into him and saw a big brown bear crushing a man dressed as a trapper. He lay huddled in the snow beneath a tall pine tree, the bear gone. I knew I was in Canada. I became aware of a Native American kneeling on one knee bending over the now still body; he seemed to be in great distress. He was bare from the waist up except for some ornaments around his upper arms. I noted the leather pants he wore, and his hair hanging loosely to his shoulders, but I could not determine if there was anything attached.

I heard him saying, "Why, oh why did you leave the path, I told you not to leave the path!"

He cried tears of grief and I felt the heaviness in his heart.

I opened my eyes to see Richard sitting quite composed before me. Even though I was relating the scenes as they came to me, he did not seem to have moved a muscle.

I shut my eyes again and immediately saw the Indian. He was standing behind my client's right shoulder in spirit-form holding a tomahawk in his hand. He was using it to chip away at my client's aura. This told me that there was something very wrong in my client's life. He had again gone off the path. The Indian told me that he would lose again if he did not return to his correct path. He asked that Richard be vigilant as there would soon be an opportunity presented that would enable him to do so. The Indian said they were souls that had traveled together many lifetimes and that they often incarnated together. This time one had agreed to serve the other by being their guide in spirit.

I had never realized before that two souls could either choose to incarnate or be a guide for the other so I was grateful for what I had learned from this session. I found that my client had also learned much when I unexpectedly met him years later.

I was traveling in the Caribbean lounging on the porch of my hotel when I heard someone say hello. I did not recognize him at all. He had longer hair, had grown a beard, and wore small wire rimmed glasses. His clothing was casual, but there was something about the energy that I recognized. He reminded me who he was then proceeded to tell me how the session we had changed his approach to life. He said that he had most definitely gone off the path and was at that time involved in illegal activities. Not long after we first met a situation had occurred that had given him the opportunity to choose to change his life without harming or interfering with anyone else. Because of the messages he received, he had moved out of his country and bought a business in the country I was now visiting. He was a model citizen, married and very happy.

PRIDE TAKES A FALL

I first heard of the case through a sister of one of my students. Phillip had been born with cystic fibrosis. He lived with his parents near Brighton on the south coast of England. I, at that time, was situated in Bristol in the west. It was arranged that I see him and his parents at the home of the sister and her doctor husband, who lived in Brighton. I made my hotel booking and set off to see my new client. The living room was the perfect place to see these new clients, as they felt completely at ease having visited the doctor and his wife socially. There was a sofa that they could sit on far enough away from the wall to allow me to stand behind them.

At first I chatted with them to put them at ease then explained how I liked to bond families when I was given the opportunity. I then asked them to place the baby between them each touching the child. I tuned in to my soul then touching each parent on the shoulder, allowed my gaze to fall on baby Phillip. In this way I could link with each soul and all three could receive the energy at once.

I felt the energy flowing through me and wondered if they felt anything at all. I realized that they were healthy, highly intelligent people, but extremely embarrassed to have a child that may not be as complete as they were. It seemed that they felt that Phillip's disability was in some way their fault.

We all enjoyed the session and they arranged for Phillip to continue receiving healing from the distance. This I did twice a week and he progressed very well. They regularly sent photos and in one it delighted me to see him standing up and looking so healthy.

When I was due to visit the United States I let them know and passed the healing on to a healer who had trained with me. It was at that time that they stopped communicating with me.

I felt sad as I had grown to love that little boy; but it is as true for me as it is for everyone, I have to let go. When I asked my student how the family was doing, I was surprised to learn that from the day her son was born, the mother had been losing her sight; and even more surprised to learn that it had been fully restored during the bonding session that day in Brighton. They had not said anything to me for they thought I must know. They also assumed similar results were common.

When we link with soul, our intention is to allow whatever is in order for the person at that time to happen. The energy for her this time was both a bonding and a healing. This allowed her to let go of the guilt she held. She had experienced herself at a deeper level than she ever had before. Prior to this session her intelligence had been of the greatest importance. With this experience, she could now choose to look at things in their true light. They were both wonderful loving parents, and I expect that they still are.

DOVEY, FAMILY TIES

I was in Phoenix to attend a Frank Alper group. I had promised that if I came to the States, I would contact a lady who had received healing from me in England. This was my first visit to the States since healing had become my calling and I kept my promise. She suggested a visit to her in Ft. Lauderdale but as it was on the other side of the States I declined through lack of funds. She asked me if I would come if she could get enough people to book healing to pay my expenses. Naturally I agreed and I met Dovey. The mother brought the baby to see me the day after I arrived in Ft. Lauderdale. Dovey was a year old and had been born with multiple handicaps. At birth he hadn't been expected to live more than a few weeks. As the mother sat holding him, I tuned into the child and saw them both in a previous incarnation. They were brother and sister and were in a hut that seemed to be on stilts. I felt that they were on an island somewhere in the Pacific. The soul that was now the mother was then a girl about 11 years old and the baby a boy of perhaps 8 or 9. The girl was saying that she could not look after the boy, and would not. She was kneeling in a corner of the hut holding a knife, both hands were wrapped around the handle, the blade pointed towards her solar plexus. The boy was frantic. He was crying uncontrollably, and I could feel the fear in him as he screamed at her, "Please don't go. I will help you."

She forced the knife into her body and as she passed from her body she could still hear him yelling, "Don't, don't, I will help you, I will help you!"

I realized that these two children had been left alone when their parents had died in the fire following either a volcanic eruption or an earthquake that had struck the island.

Two weeks later I led a seminar and not only were the mother and baby there, but so was the baby's grandmother. Grandmother turned out to be the mother who had died in the fire on the island.

During the seminar I had everyone follow a releasing meditation and they were all quiet listening to my words as I guided them through it.

The grandmother quite calmly said, "I'm on fire, I'm on fire!"

No one paid any attention at first as they thought she meant inside herself due to the releasing. I had to specifically ask someone 'to please put the lady's fire out'.

She had backed up to a candle and her dress had caught fire. Her daughter immediately dropped the baby and rushed to her mother's aid. This time the fire did not get her!

This lady has never really cleared her fear of fire, and admits that it is so frightening to her that she won't even let herself think about it.

What I realized was that the girl on the island was very spoiled and had become self-centered. She did not want to look after herself, let alone her brother. The boy screaming he would help her was so sincere that when she reincarnated he chose to reincarnate in a way that would be most beneficial to teach her to serve others. She already had three healthy children when he was born, and at that time they had enough money to employ someone to take a lot of the responsibility of the every day caring from her.

The father died when the baby was 4 years old and the money supply dried up. Now there was no father to share the load and no money to employ anyone to help her. Slowly she had been taking more and more responsibility as they moved to a different area causing a complete change in lifestyle.

So once again everything is perfect in it's time, and the baby lived to be six years old. He was a beautiful loving soul and although he could not communicate by speech he could certainly indicate to you what he liked and disliked. He is free of his little body now and I am aware that he was involved in teaching something to all of us whose lives he touched. He never walked, talked, sat up or ate solid food, yet he was mischievous, full of fun and loving.

He came through a medium recently thanking me for asking the Dolphins to take charge of him. He said they are still looking after him. He also thanked me for looking after his mother.

A very special soul who chose to serve.

THE ACCEPTANCE OF POWER

At last we were getting somewhere! It is so hard at times to get beyond the belief systems to the underlying cause of a problem. It seems that the more one tries to destroy these systems the more resistance is felt.

Susan had first come with a lump in her chest and heaviness in her left leg and foot. I was feeling that the lump in her chest was emotional tension, and as I looked at her I saw the tears coming into her eyes. I realized she knew that I had felt it, and the relief of someone sharing the feeling had caused the tears.

She was experiencing the re-occurrence of an old behavior pattern, and as I tuned into her I described to her how she felt during her behavior.

Susan was a powerful person, yet when she was with a man she found she herself acting as though she had no power at all. She didn't like herself for it. In fact, even as she was in the middle of acting powerless she knew it was an act and disliked herself for not being able to stop.

I saw her as a male in the garden of Hampton Court Palace in England. This was the home of Henry the Eighth and I believe Elizabeth 1st. I knew that he, my client, had a lot of power and used it to his own end. He was dressed in the finery of the times, and I instinctively knew that he was trusted by most of the people in the court. I then saw him dressed in a puce robe whispering into someone's ear. Whatever it was that he had whispered had caused a lot of people to end up in prison or to be executed. He himself ended up in the Tower of London, but not until he was much older.

The experience of this life of misused power, would lead the soul to choose a life lesson involving power. When she incarnated this time she reproduced the fear of being in power and acted accordingly, trying to avoid misuse by giving her power away. This would continue until she had worked her way through it. Situations were created where she would be truly tested. This was all at an unconscious level.

Now she had got to the point in her life where she was experiencing a certain amount of abuse. A lump was created in her chest to give her the opportunity to release old energies, so having recently heard of our healing method, chose to put herself through the healing process. As soon as she was strong enough to handle the truth, and the change this would bring, the memory surfaced to be dealt with. She had her healing session, and as well as removing the lump in her chest, the feeling of a boot on her left leg and foot were removed. Now she could take on the responsibility of life and moving forward in her own power.

Margarite Westo

THE BIG SNAKE

Ellen lived nearby. She originally came to me for a healing session. This was an unusual occurrence as some of the locals looked on me as some weird magical person to be feared. Being a small village, the rest really didn't want to be seen coming to me because of what the other people would think. Ellen had been very pleased with the outcome of her healing and as a result had called me in when her husband had a stroke. I worked a couple of times a week with him at their home until he was better. At times Ellen even attended our meditation evenings. Knowing how positively she considered her experience of healing, imagine my surprise when she started to ignore me when we met in a store or in the lane leading up from the village. It was some time before I found out that the church that she and her husband attended had put the idea in her head that healing was from the devil, and that the people that performed it were witches. The power the church had over them was so strong that they could not even believe their own experience. They lived in fear of hell, and therefore they were living in it!

I thank God that nothing is wasted when it comes to healing. At some point each one will feel the pull of the soul towards the Divine truth, and healing always helps towards this time.

Ellen had a cousin Gwyneth who lived some considerable distance away in Wales, and during the time she and her husband were still receiving healing they had told her about their sessions and how wonderful they felt. Gwyneth was of the same religious discipline, and attended her local branch of the church in Wales.

It was about a year later that Gwyneth became strangely ill and went to see her doctor. This lady preferred homeopathic to allopathic medicine and after a long interview her doctor prescribed what he considered to be the appropriate remedy for her. He had examined her and although she felt and appeared to be quite ill, there seemed to be no organic reason. Gwyneth followed the doctor's instructions to the letter, and was shocked to wake up one morning, soon after taking the remedy, with the definite mark of an enormous bite on her body, just as though she had been attacked. This lady knew that she had not been attacked, so she decided to go back to the doctor. In despair she told him what had appeared on her body, and asked him if she was losing her mind. He examined the mark and came to the conclusion that the nearest creature that he could see leaving a bite like that was a dog. He still didn't feel satisfied. It came into his mind that it was something to do with a past life experience, but had no way of knowing what.

It seems that previously in his practice he had seen past life energies being released when he treated his patients with homeopathic remedies. I was given to understand that this was the first time he had come across such a definite mark! Somewhere he had heard of my work, so he suggested that she make an appointment to come to the center to see if there was anything I could do for her.

Gwyneth realized that she was being given the name of the same healer that her cousin had attended. As this was the second time she had heard of me, she took it as a sign that I could help her. At this time she had not heard from Ellen what the church had decreed, as Ellen was now frightened to even mention my name.

When she called to make the appointment she mentioned that she had heard of me from both her cousin Ellen, and her doctor. I didn't know what to expect for I had not yet found out why Ellen was ignoring me.

As I opened the door to her I was confronted by a little woman of no more than 5 feet, very round, wearing a navy blue day dress which was so long I could hardly see her ankles. It had a large stark white collar of lace. She wore no makeup, and her hair was cut in a style making her look very stern.

She was very tense; I could feel the anxiety sitting like a big lump in her chest area. As I brought her into the house I offered her a cup of tea to relax her. She declined and I took her straight to the healing room. I had hardly sat her in the chair opposite me when I was transported to a river in the jungle battling with the biggest snake I had ever seen. I felt myself in the body of young woman. I tried to free myself but the body of the snake was about 24 inches around. It was coiling itself around my body and I knew it would crush the life out of me, as I was so frail in comparison. There was jungle all around and I felt that I was totally alone. I continued to struggle and I could feel the panic surging through my body. Then suddenly I was outside the body and I saw the creature suddenly loosen it's coils, open it's mouth and wrap it's jaw around this young woman just above the waist over the lower ribs. It's mouth was so wide when it was open that it reached from above her hip to just past her belly button. Whether it had teeth or not didn't really matter, the jaw was so strong it crushed her ribs and her spine. She then mercifully fainted, and the creature went on to devour her.

Up to this point I did not know why Gwyneth had come to me, only that a doctor had recommended that she come. I had assumed that she was physically ill, how wrong we can be when we make assumptions. I felt compelled to describe to her what I was experiencing, as it happened. At the same time another part of me was aware of her shock at what I was saying. I must admit that yet another part of me was wondering what her reaction was going to be. Would she just get up and walk out?

I had only been working at this depth of consciousness for about 8 years when I saw her, and although this may seem sufficient time to become accustomed to the work, I had not the benefits of all the experience I have now.

What Gwyneth actually did was start to release by crying uncontrollably. I could feel the healing energies going to her as I sat feeding her tissue after tissue. Eventually she settled down enough to tell me about the mark. It was exactly where I had seen the jaw closing on the body. We then, through a healing session released all of the past energies of the experience without her going through the agony of re-experiencing the trauma of it. This left her feeling free and joyous. It left me marveling at the whole procedure of soul path clearing. I explained to her that healing does not stop with the end of the session, and would continue for a couple of days. I told her to rest and to allow it to work and to help regain the strength she had used going through an emotional release and a change of energy.

This change always needs time to be assimilated. I asked her to let me know how she got on, as sometimes the continued healing can bring to the surface unexpected memories and feelings. These I could help with without her coming to see me if she asked.

Gwyneth called me a few days later to tell me the mark had disappeared from her body. When she awoke the morning after the session it had gone. It had disappeared as quickly as it had appeared. She was feeling good, and I never heard from her again. A shame, I forgot to ask her if she had been afraid of snakes!

THE BLINDMAN

When my husband and I moved to the house in Bristol, the passage leading from the front door to the staircase, which ascended directly in front of you, was very narrow. The carved post at the bottom of the banisters was ornate and protruded as the passage turned to the left. We could do nothing more than put my piano in the only room situated before that turn, the healing room.

Normally I do not have anything in the healing room other than the furniture and healing aids necessary for seeing clients, and nothing is done in there but meditation and healing. I have found that if you keep a very clear energy in your healing space, the patient instinctively feels less vulnerable and the acceptance of the healing is much deeper as the sacred energy builds up.

Once we had moved in we started renovating the house. Within a couple of months it had progressed to the point where I started to receive people for healing three days a week.

With the move my piano needed tuning. This was on my mind when I stopped to look at a doctors examination table I noticed was for sale as I drove through town. As I returned to my car I saw a small van with piano tuner painted on the side. No one was around so I took down the phone number and continued on my way. When I got home I called and made an appointment through his wife, so I did not have any contact with him before he arrived to tune the piano.

It surprised me to see he had a guide dog, which he promptly tied to the piano leg. I asked how he had traveled as I was confused about the van. He told me his wife drove the van as an advertisement and he went everywhere by bus. He then proceeded to tune my piano. I left them alone in the healing room and later returned to see if I could bring either of them a drink.

He said he felt that the atmosphere he was working in was different to anything that he had felt before, and asked me what happened in that room. I tried my best to explain what I did without seeming too way out, and he asked me if he could come for a healing. He stressed that he would not come unless I promised not to tell his wife. He didn't want it to get back to his church for they thought healing was from the devil.

It really is no business of mine how people act in their lives so I agreed. I explained to him that I couldn't divulge anything that happened in the healing sessions for ethical reasons; he decided to make an appointment.

When he arrived at the appointed time, I did not give him a chance to tell me why he had wanted to come for healing as I felt an urgency in his energy just to get on with the healing. So I wasted no time in getting him onto the healing table and tuned into his energies.

He opened very quickly and I was instantly aware of a previous incarnation where I saw him gouging peoples eyes out with what looked like rags tied onto the end of a thick stick dipped in some sort of oil substance. He was dipping the stick in the fire to light it. He then turned and plunged it into the eyes of the helpless men, one after another.

The screams I heard were terrible and I knew that the blind piano tuner had chosen to be born sightless to experience the effects he had caused others to live with. I felt that he looked at his disability as a punishment. I later found that the church he attended preached hell fire and damnation so he had chosen a double lesson.

1. Not to give his power away, in this case to his church.
2. Believe your own experience rather than the interpretation of another's.

He told me about the session, describing more or less the same scene as I had seen, and he said that as the session went on he started to feel more and more at peace. He then experienced seeing color inside his eyelids, this gradually turned to white light. The rest of the healing he didn't remember much of at all, as he had gone deeper into his consciousness; but he felt he had been there hours.

A few days later I had a phone call from him to thank me. He told me that he had been having a hearing problem and the pain had plagued him for years. That had been what had prompted him to make the appointment. According to the hospital it had been caused by a series of abscesses in his ears which they had been unsuccessful in curing. Now he was going to let me know if he had anymore abscesses. He told me that the most wonderful thing he got from the healing was an understanding, that he was feeling more at peace than at any other time in his life.

I suggested that he forget looking for any abscesses and just let go of the concern for his health and then he would be sure to stay healthy. He didn't have any more pain in his ears, at least for the three years I was in touch with him.

He remained blind, as he had chosen to learn through his life of sightlessness, but he found peace in the realization that it was not an angry God that was punishing him, in fact it wasn't a punishment at all.

THE THREE

A friend's friend, Jimmy couldn't seem to get to me. First he had the flu and had to cancel his appointment, then his car wouldn't start and he had to cancel another appointment. He was determined so we made another appointment. As I wasn't actually living or working in the area at this time, I arranged to see him at a location away from where I was staying. I had originally agreed to see him as a favor to Katie, an old client, so I hoped he could get to me this time.

I arrived in good time to prepare the room and to meditate then proceeded to wait for his arrival. As the time went by I wondered if he was going to turn up at all for he was very late. Then the phone rang. It was Katie, Jimmy had lost himself and had not taken my phone number with him. He was somewhere on the Florida turnpike in spite of the fact that it was a straight drive up I95 from Miami.

Somehow he had taken the wrong lane and had to follow the traffic, which at that point led onto the turnpike. I gave the directions and went back to waiting. I was not going to be able to give him the full time as I had an appointment at another location afterward.

Jimmy finally arrived, and I was surprised to see that he was as calm as he was, considering his ordeal. I asked him to remove his shoes before entering the healing room and proceeded to go in before him.

He was a very large man and it seemed he would completely fill the armed chair he had lowered himself into. It was now that the stress started to show itself, so I turned the tape on to record the session and started by teaching him the breathing technique for relaxing and centering his energies. He found it hard to do and we didn't have the time to practice for long so I asked him to practice at home by following the instructions on the tape. As I tuned into his soul I saw him as an artist and because of the clothing I knew it was a different life. He was young and slender man with a clear complexion and dark hair. There were two other young men with him, also artists and around the same age. It was obvious that they were in a three-way relationship and I felt a lot of jealousy between the other two. They were all very talented artists each with a particular flair for color.

I returned to this life knowing he had brought his artist's eye in with him. I asked him what he did. He told me he was a photographer, and yes, he had a good eye for composition. I became aware of a smoke screen all along one side of him and at first could not tell where it was coming from. If it originated from him, I knew it meant that he was not willing to face something; if it originated from someone else, then they were holding him back.

It was then that I saw one of the two souls who had been artists with him. In this life he was his father, now deceased. I found that the cloud originated from Jimmy himself. He was not willing to face the completion he needed with his father. We discussed this and how even though his father was no longer living, he could still complete by a method of visualization and interaction called 'Cutting the Links'. This would not only allow his father's soul freedom to 'go on', but would also free him.

He drew an envelope out of his pocket passing it to me. He asked if I could help him by telling him what I felt from the vibrations, as he was confused. I held it in my hand and closed my eyes. I had been careful to only look at the reverse side of the envelope, as I did not want to be influenced by the writing or the postmark. I immediately saw a young woman and a strong relationship, which would be very colorful. As I received the impressions of the vivid and brilliant reds, blues, purples and greens, I knew this was the third artist from the previous life.

I opened my eyes and realized how hungry he was for this relationship, but at the same time was not ready to make a commitment. I saw that he had previously been working to clear out a lot of old energies. This was yet another situation to be experienced, then cleared to aid his soul growth. Here was evidence yet again of how growth is acquired by souls incarnating and playing the parts required, how we serve each other by interaction.

I brought the session to a close. He asked me to let him know when I would be in Florida again as he would like to have another session, and I felt that he would understand himself a little better from this short time spent together. I also knew why he had created so many obstacles to our meeting. Next time there would be no need for obstacles as he would have found that to face himself was not as bad as he had instinctively thought. In fact here was a very talented loving man, who had learned that he was not only on the receiving end of other soul's playacting, but was himself playing different parts for different people to serve them.

SEX, WHAT A MESS!

This was Rachel's second session. As I tuned into her I could see that her energy was completely different from when I had first seen her. Her original visit was to help her get over the fear of losing the first love she had tentatively allowed into her life. For some time she had been experiencing pain in her chest. No tests had found a physical reason for it. A friend suggested she come to see me when her partner informed her that he did not want to continue with the relationship. They were still together as nothing was decided yet.

On that visit, while she was on the healing couch, we released, with her soul's guidance, an energy block from the heart chakra. It was after that Rachel felt loved for the first time in her life. She had never felt love from anyone before, including her mother. This didn't mean that she hadn't been loved, just that the energy block had been causing her to reject it, no matter where it came from.

When Rachel arrived for her second visit she told me that she had been feeling a lot better and had not had the pain in the chest at all, and no, her partner had not left.

As I got her to center her energies using the breathing technique, I started tuning into her through the balloon method. I found that the heart area was indeed better but now the solar plexus (3rd) and the root chakra (1st) were both very depleted. I picked up that there were two reasons for this. One was that her mind was going over and over the same thing, and the other that other life experiences were surfacing to be dealt with. Both were creating negative energy which needed dealing with.

I saw an Arab riding through the desert and knew that this nomad traveled alone. He visited with families and tribes as he traveled about without becoming attached to any of them. I was not given any explanation, but knew that Rachel was that same soul. As I continued to look at the energies her soul was putting out to me, I noticed that there was a problem to do with sex.

I asked her if she had anything to tell me about her sexual experience. Rachel told me that she thought she loved her husband and had wanted to have sex with him. Sex was not satisfactory, as she always felt like she was being violated and tensed up when they were together. She therefore experienced a lot of pain during intercourse. Although her husband had been patient and very understanding, this was one of the things that had caused their relationship to suffer, and no wonder!

As I felt myself being pulled deeper into her energies I saw a girl about twelve years old being led into a hall by her mother. She was dressed in a pretty white dress and had flowers in her curly blonde hair. Her mother led her to the middle of the room, then turned and left the way she had come. The room appeared to be a banqueting hall with long tables on three sides. There were no women at all in the hall, and the men were drunk and rowdy. One of the men climbed over the table and pushed the girl to the wooden floor. All of the men seemed to be big, heavy soldiers and this one was no exception. He pulled her dress up and undoing his own trousers he proceeded to rape her, laughing as he did. Before he had finished another man was ready to take his place. This continued with the girl crying and sometimes screaming, but the more she screamed the heartier the men laughed. There was now more than one man at a time with her. They were sodomizing her, venting their sexual energy in her mouth and her ears, and relieving themselves over her body. The girl's screams had become a whimper as the lifeblood left her. And so she died, and still they continued to rape her, not seeming to realize that the life had left the little body that lay in it's growing pool of blood.

This life ending was the reason for the soul choosing a male incarnation in the Arabian life that I had seen. Another female existence would have been too painful an experience for her to go through again. He choose the nomadic life so that he would not be obligated to have a close relationship that would lead to a sexual encounter and so remained celibate throughout his life. Although he did not heal the sexual energy in that lifetime, he did learn to be alone and his inner strength grew.

Having gained strength the soul had chosen a female incarnation again. Now Rachel's aim was to learn the difference between love and lust, and to experience the sharing of love. To do this the fear had to be overcome by life experience and healing.

At the first session Rachel had been talking to me about *having sex,* but after the second healing I was delighted to hear her talking about *making love*. The fact that she now referred to the sexual act as making love, to me, appeared to be a great step forward.

If we do not release the pain of a situation as we experience it, we take it with us in the form of energy when we pass on. Although I was not shown the life that caused the child's sexual experience, I am led to believe that it would have been one of a male. No doubt he would have used his power to domineer and abuse women. From that the soul would have chosen to experience the abuse he had laid on others, explaining the child's life experience. The energy we are born with, being magnetic attracts to it like energies. We do this in order to progress. If we don't have any indication that there is something to address, how can we address it? If in a previous incarnation this soul had created the opportunity to let go of the energies to do with its misuse of the sexual energy, it would not have attracted the energy of rape.

Now Rachel realizing that there was really nothing wrong with her, hoped that she could show her partner that she had healed. Her desire was for a lasting relationship and she hoped her change in behavior would lead to exactly that.

DON'T CARRY THAT RESTRICTION WITH YOU

This time we were definitely getting to the root of the trouble! I had been sending transfer healing on an irregular basis since I had attended Alex's birth five years before.

Alex was born with the cord wrapped around his neck making it difficult for him to take his first breath. He was purple and the midwife did what she had to do, but still he was reluctant to breathe. We both concentrated the healing energies towards him to bring his consciousness into this world, and at last he breathed. Considering the length of time between leaving the womb and breathing I was surprised he was not damaged at all.

His mother and father separated early in his life and his upbringing has been shared between them ever since. There had been times when the child had been seen to be vicious to his mother in ways that would be hard to imagine. Other times he had expressed hate and his behavior had not been what would normally be expected of one so inexperienced in life.

I had been asked to give Alex a weekly healing, this would be the fourth session. Normally for a child of this age I do a fifteen-minute session. I like one of the parents to be with them gently touching them in some way. This time the father would be with Alex who would be asleep at the time.

I started in the usual way, linking with Alex's soul with healing intention. Before long I was aware that there was a feeling on his upper body that I knew was the memory of a straight jacket. For a moment I felt stuck. I found myself quietly asking where I should start taking it off. I didn't hear a reply but started pulling it off from the top. It was very strong and it took quite a while. I knew that the room he had been in was dark and that he was there because he had been violent to others.

As I continued the healing I realized that he really wanted to clear these past energies. At soul level he had chosen these two people as parents and the situation between them, knowing they would help him to bring the energy of the experience to the surface to be dealt with and released.

The healing this time actually took one hour and fifteen minutes.

The next day the father called me and I told him what had happened at my end. He then told me that he had to concentrate on keeping the boy still, for although he did not wake up, he tossed and turned and nearly fell off the bed. He then started speaking loud enough for the father to hear. He clearly heard him say, "Start from the top." This was the first time that I had a witness to a conversation in a transfer healing.

I realized that this session had released and changed the old confusing energies of violence for the boy, and it was obvious that he needed to continue receiving healing. It was a few years before the cause of his birth experience surfaced.

At this later session, as I went deeper into the transfer healing energy, I was being taken into the energy of darkness. This energy felt thick, and as I attempted to see where I was going I became aware of something swinging in the distance. As I got closer I realized it was this soul's body in another incarnation hanging from a gallows. Now I found myself releasing the body and clearing the neck of the memory. It was only after closing the session that I realized that the cord around the neck at his birth had been caused by the cellular memory of the rope.

Today he is a very creative, intelligent, loving and compassionate human being. I am sure that his soul's choice to evolve will bring more memories to the surface at times, I am confident that he will be able to deal with them himself. Already I have seen evidence of a memory of a concentration camp experience rising through his poetry.

With every healing I do, I am reinforcing the fact that there are no limits to what we can do for ourselves, as well as others, if we can just release all beliefs. Beliefs create illusions that appear to be real, like the story of the emperor and his belief that his clothes were invisible. Once you let go of the beliefs and aim at the experience of God, or reality, your life will start to come into line with what your soul has intended for you. As you clear out the old pattern you become freer, for now you are not obligated to follow anything. You only have to allow!

Margarite Westo

THE BALLOON METHOD

This is a transcription of the balloon method as used in that first session and found myself repeating at every soul path session from then on.

"First take a few deep breaths to relax."

I paused to give him time to relax into the breathing.

"Now as you continue to breathe I would like you to close your eyes and keep focusing on your breathing. I will direct you in bringing all of your energies, past, present, and future, into a center point. I want you to be aware of my words, I do not want you to focus on them, keep your focus on your breathing, as long as you are aware of my words you will bring all of your energies to a center point. It is easy, you do not have to visualize anything, or try to do anything, you just have to be aware of my words." ...pause... *"with every in breath, I want you to know that the energy is creating a chamber near your heart, in the heart center. This chamber will become larger with each breath, and more filled with this beautiful energy. As you continue to breathe knowing that this is occurring, above your head there is a big bunch of balloons, all different colors."*

I continued.

"Each balloon represents something of you, it may be your conception or your birth, it may be your mother or your father, a feeling, a thought, either sad or happy. Everything you have experienced is there, every thought, every feeling, every soul you have encountered along the way, every action and every reaction, all there on individual balloons. So you see it is a very big bunch of balloons. Also there is the present day, your situation now, the people in your life now, your health. What we know as the future is there also. Amongst it all is your core being, that part of you that is your soul, your spirit, your light body. That part of you that is co-creator with God, that part of you that is the only thing in the universe that knows what is right for you."

I paused again...

"As you continue to breathe the chamber in your heart center has become quite large enough to accommodate all of your balloons. I would like you to allow them to drift down one by one and enter that chamber where they will be nurtured by the energy and where I will be able to see what it is that your soul is having us work with today. So continuing to breathe nice and slowly, allow these balloons to drift down one by one, I will now be quiet for a few moments to observe."

Margarite Westo

I paused for only a few moments.

"O.K. you can relax now, you can open your eyes if you want to. The first thing I see is…"

I then described the scenes as the balloons appeared and explained how they related to his present condition. I saw what each one represented and instinctively knew the story attached to it. As I spoke of this to the client, I witnessed the color of the balloon changing as the energy was cleared.

Owl Meets Alien
Amongst Others On My Soul's Journey

IF I SHOULD LEAVE BEFORE YOU SAY GOODBYE

If I should leave before you say goodbye,
Just let me go in peace and please don't cry,
Remember me and know I now am free.

Free of the worldly struggle and the pain,
My body gone, my memories still remain,
Beyond all doubt and now my light shines out.

It seems like all the stresses of my life
Have worked together just to set me free,
Along with gains made that were not explained
When I was earthbound, and just being me.

If I could choose to live my life again,
Or take my chances on some other plain,
I do believe I would return to earth,
Its beauty and its lessons to attain.

The souls I'd met I'd want to meet again,
I'd like to love, and write, and paint, and dance.
In truth I left so many things undone
I realize now I need another chance.

So if I leave without those last goodbyes,
Do not be sad, rejoice to know there's choice,
Then make your choices knowing lives are short,
Complete your dreams, speak truth, let's hear your voice.

Margarite Westo

Now 'til we meet again some place, somewhere,
A time when it is right our lives to share,
I leave my gratitude and blessings to
Please know that I will always cherish you.
Margarite

ABOUT THE AUTHOR

Born in London, England in 1933, Margarite experienced her "spiritual awakening" in 1970. After some reluctance, she started her path of healing. Margarite channeled Transfer healing, a method of distance healing through the soul. In 1980, she moved with her husband to Bristol and started the first of three centers. Here Margarite found she was gifted with the ability to recall people's other life experiences and how they affected everyday life. In 1987, she separated from her husband; created Future Way, her healing business; studied with Frank Alper; and accepted an invite to work in Florida. Margarite returned to Florida the following year and eventually relocating to the United States. Her present center is in Asheville, North Carolina.

Printed in the United States
32662LVS00007B/265-369